INTRODUCTION TO MONEY LAUNDERING DETERRENCE

The Chartered Institute for Securities & Investment

Mission Statement:

> *To set standards of professional excellence and integrity for the investment and securities industry, providing qualifications and promoting the highest level of competence to our members, other individuals and firms.*

Formerly the Securities & Investment Institute (SII), and originally founded by members of the London Stock Exchange in 1992, the Institute is the leading examining, membership and awarding body for the securities and investment industry. We were awarded a royal charter in October 2009, becoming the Chartered Institute for Securities & Investment. We currently have around 40 000 members who benefit from a programme of professional and social events, with continuing professional development (CPD) and the promotion of integrity, very much at the heart of everything we do. Additionally, more than 40 000 examinations are taken annually in more than 50 countries throughout the world.

The CISI also currently works with a number of academic institutions offering qualifications, membership and exemptions as well as information on careers in financial services. We have over 40 schools and colleges offering our introductory qualifications and have 7 University Centres of Excellence recognised by the CISI as offering leadership in academic education on financial markets.

You can contact us through our website www.cisi.org

Our membership believes that keeping up to date is central to professional development. We are delighted to endorse the Wiley/CISI publishing partnership and recommend this series of books to our members and all those who work in the industry.

As part of the CISI CPD Scheme, reading relevant financial publications earns members of the Chartered Institute for Securities & Investment the appropriate number of CPD hours under the Self-Directed learning category. For further information, please visit www.cisi.org/cpdscheme

Ruth Martin
Managing Director

INTRODUCTION TO MONEY LAUNDERING DETERRENCE

Dennis Cox

Risk Reward Ltd, London, UK

WILEY

A John Wiley & Sons, Ltd., Publication

This edition first published 2011

Registered office
John Wiley & Sons Ltd, The Atrium, Southern Gate, Chichester, West Sussex, PO19 8SQ, United Kingdom

For details of our global editorial offices, for customer services and for information about how to apply for permission to reuse the copyright material in this book please see our website at www.wiley.com. The right of the author to be identified as the author of this work has been asserted in accordance with the Copyright, Designs and Patents Act 1988.

Library of Congress Cataloging-in-Publication Data

Cox, Dennis W.
Introduction to money laundering deterrence / Dennis Cox.
p. cm.
ISBN 978-0-470-06572-3
1. Money laundering. 2. Money laundering—Prevention. 3. Terrorism—Finance. 4. Terrorism—Prevention. I. Title.
HV8079.M64C69 2010
364.16′8—dc22

2010031108

A catalogue record for this book is available from the British Library.

ISBN 978-0470-06572-3

Typeset in 10/12pt Trump Medieval by Toppan Best-set Premedia Limited
Printed and bound in Great Britain by TJ International Ltd, Padstow, Cornwall

CONTENTS

ABOUT THE AUTHOR

Dennis William Cox, BSc FCSI FCA is a leading financial services risk management and internal audit specialist and CEO of Risk Reward Limited, a risk management, internal audit consulting firm serving banks, regulators and financial institutions in developed and emerging markets based in London, UK.

He has held senior management positions within the banking and accountancy profession as Director, Risk Management at HSBC Insurance Brokers Limited, and Director, Risk Management, Prudential Portfolio Managers. Formerly he held a number of roles within the audit profession including Senior Audit Manager (Compliance) at HSBC Holdings PLC and Senior Manager (Banking and Finance) at both BDO Binder Hamlyn and Arthur Young.

Dennis is a Fellow, Co-founder and Chairman of the Risk Forum for the Chartered Institute for Securities & Investment. A Fellow of the Institute of Chartered Accountants (FCA), he has also been a National Council Member for 15 years. He holds a BSc Honours degree in Mathematics from London University.

Dennis is an accomplished international conference chairman and lecturer, and is the author of a number of publications including *Banking and Finance: Accounts, Audit and Practice* (Butterworths, 1993), *The Mathematics of Banking and Finance* (Wiley, 2006) and *Frontiers of Risk Management* (Euromoney, 2007).

INTRODUCTION

This book sets itself the simple objective of providing the reader with sufficient information to enable them to understand the key issues that relate to two of the largest problems faced by financial institutions today: money laundering deterrence and terrorist financing.

This is an introductory text, providing outline information to enable the key issues to be understood and the regulatory framework appreciated. Since the market for money laundering and terrorist financing is by its nature global, so is this text. Consequently whilst different rules and regulations are implemented into local legislation, it is the global standards which underpin all of these local requirements. Consequently such global standards as exist at the time of writing this text are included within the book. If you require detailed rules and regulations regarding a specific market there are other texts that you should refer to.

There is a lot of money laundering around and prosecutions are increasing. A couple of recent examples are as follows:

Wisconsin (USA) Restaurant Owner Sentenced to 48 Months for Structuring Financial Transactions

On September 21, 2009, in Madison, Wis., the owner of a restaurant in Baraboo, Wisconsin, was sentenced to 48 months in prison for money laundering offences related to the structuring of financial transactions. According to court documents, the restaurant owner borrowed $616 726 from a regular customer of his restaurant. He instructed the customer to write the checks in small amounts so that he could use them to pay food distributors. However, he actually negotiated the checks for cash. He drove to multiple banks and multiple branches of the same bank to deposit the cash and avoid having currency transaction reports generated by the banks for cash transactions exceeding $10 000, to avoid the money laundering being detected. Additionally, he also had associates cash other checks and return the proceeds to him.

In this case the crime is fraud and the restaurant owner is seeking to use the financial systems to enable him to make full use of the monies. In money laundering there is always some form of criminal activity – who would need to disguise legitimate funds? Often it is the nature of the funds which determines the approach that is likely to be adopted. Here we have a fraudster using multiple bank accounts to attempt to disguise the source of funds. As we shall see in subsequent chapters there are many criminal activities and also many forms of money laundering.

(*Source:* http://www.irs.gov/compliance/enforcement/article/0,,id=187285,00.html)

Sometimes the investigations undertaken by the crime agencies can result in successful prosecution as shown by this press release from the UK's Serious Organised Crime Agency (SOCA):

Suspected heroin trafficker Mark Brown captured in the Netherlands

18 December 2009

Forty-four year old Mark Ronald Brown was arrested by Amsterdam Regional Police on Thursday afternoon at a petrol station in Almere on the outskirts of Amsterdam. (17th December 2009)

Brown is believed to have been the head of an organised crime gang responsible for the importation of hundreds of kilos of heroin into the UK. He was captured following an operation involving SOCA and the Dutch police.

Details of his status as a wanted fugitive had been publicised through Crimestoppers 'Operation Captura', something which Brown alluded to when arrested. He commented that he had felt unsafe in Spain knowing that he was wanted there, and so had moved to the

Netherlands. He added that, now that he had been arrested, he was glad that it was all over.

A SOCA spokesman said: "This arrest is a massive endorsement for Crimestoppers Operation Captura and its reputation in the criminal community. SOCA and our international partners, working together with Crimestoppers and the general public, are having a real impact on UK fugitives abroad - making sure they realise that at any moment there could be a knock on the door followed by the clink of handcuffs."

Source: http://www.soca.gov.uk/news/154-suspected-heroin-trafficker-mark-brown-captured-in-the-netherlands

Clearly international contacts are also required to detect major money laundering rings. Another press release from the Serious Organised Crime Agency highlights this clearly:

International Money Launderer Arrested

07 December 2009

Naresh Jain, the subject of a long term investigation by SOCA and international partners, was arrested in New Delhi on Sunday morning (06 December 2009). Jain is alleged to have controlled a worldwide money laundering system that, at its height, was capable of moving $2.2bn a year.

Jain, who is banned from entering the UK, was arrested in Dubai in 2007 by Dubai Police as part of a year long joint investigation between SOCA, the Dubai Police and the Italian Guardia di Finanza, but fled to India while awaiting trial. SOCA subsequently worked closely with the Dubai and Indian authorities to assist them with their enquiries. Jain is currently in custody in India and SOCA are liaising with both Indian and Dubai police on the next steps.

Commenting on the arrest, SOCA Deputy Director Ian Cruxton said:

This operation is part of SOCA's long term strategy targeting specialist money launderers based overseas. The illegal money transfer systems they use provide the infrastructure to launder cash for organised crime groups whose activities directly impact on the United Kingdom.

These networks pay no attention to cultural or geographical barriers. They launder money for organised crime groups from any ethnic background or criminal business, particularly UK, Pakistani and Turkish Nationals based in the UK and mainland Europe involved in drugs trafficking.

SOCA continues to share intelligence and work with international partners to create a hostile environment for criminals both domestically and internationally.

This book aims to provide all bank employees with the basic information that they need to be part of the global attempt to identify and prosecute those involved in money laundering or terrorist financing, whilst explaining the key terms and associated risks. It should be part of an education and awareness campaign conducted throughout the financial institution to raise people's knowledge of key requirements and expectations, ensuring that each firm complies with the local rules and regulations promulgated in their jurisdiction by their relevant authority. In the course of the following chapters we shall explain some of the approaches that a bank needs to adopt to deter money laundering and to enable terrorist financing to be identified.

Where possible or relevant we have included references to relevant rules and regulations within the body of the book, where the reader may find additional information if required.

In writing any book the author needs a good team around them. In this case my colleagues at Risk Reward Limited and in particular Gurmeet Rathor have provided both content and assistance throughout the development of this book. Without their help this book would never have been completed.

I do hope that you find this helpful and comprehensive and remember that if you are working for a bank and money laundering or terrorist financing have not yet been found – it does not mean that it is not around. It just means that you have not found it yet.

Dennis Cox
Risk Reward Limited
London

Chapter 1

WHAT IS MONEY LAUNDERING?

THE INITIAL CONCERNS

The industry which we refer to as money laundering has developed significantly over recent years. The concerns originally started with a key public concern over organised crime and the negative impact that this was having on people. The thought existed that by tracking the movement of cash, the relevant authorities would be able to detect patterns of behaviour to enable them to identify organised crime though its use of the financial sector. The key element being that such funds would be moved within the banking system to disguise the original source of the funds, enabling organised crime to make free use of funds that initially may have originated from tainted sources including drug trafficking.

The original drive to have money laundering legislation in any country always comes from some form of issue which is considered to be of such magnitude that it actually gets onto the political agenda. The legislation is then generally developed in a hurry to meet these perceived and specific needs. The initial drive to have money laundering deterrence of what were essentially narcotic-related issues has now extended in most countries to include terrorist financing and then finally to any illegal act.

The consequence of the manner in which legislation has been enacted is that what are considered to be money laundering predicate offences do vary considerably between countries. More recently there has been a significant effort to achieve a level of international standardisation within the money laundering deterrence arena, led by groups such as the Financial Actions Task Force (FATF), as discussed in Chapter 2, although they of course do not have any statutory responsibility. It still remains the responsibility of the local legislature to implement the requirements into local law – and they will often take into account specific local issues and other existing legislation in doing so. This is particularly the case in the USA, as discussed in Chapter 7.

WHAT IS MONEY LAUNDERING?

The idea of money laundering is simple in principle. The person who has received some form of ill gotten gains will seek to ensure that they can use these funds without people realising that they are the result of inappropriate behaviour. To do this they will need to disguise the proceeds such that the original source of the proceeds is hidden and therefore the funds themselves appear to be legitimate. Given that it was often cash that was needed to be disguised, then the criminal would often seek out legitimate cash-based businesses to enable them to disguise the source of their illegitimate cash.

By mingling legitimate and illegitimate funds the entire amount could potentially appear to be legitimate, and therefore laundered. Indeed launderettes which were generally cash-based businesses would represent an ideal business which might be used to achieve this. Laundering money has two main connotations. It both refers to the use of a cash business such as a launderette to facilitate the mingling of legal and illegal funds; while it also refers to the generic process of disguising the original proceeds of the funds.

If a business normally takes in cash of say £20 000 per week, would anyone notice if this increased to £25 000? The original £20 000 is legitimate business that is being conducted, whereas the next £5000 may represent funds from an inappropriate source that is being laundered through the medium of the legitimate business. Mingling legitimate and illegitimate funds is a typical basis on which a money launderer may choose to operate. You do need to recognise that there are two main styles of money laundering – professional and amateur. The professional money launderer will take advantage of any perceived weakness in the systems of control operated by a financial institution or structure. Amateur money laundering takes an opportunity and does not really cover its tracks very well. It is normally the latter type of money laundering that is detected. The professional is always much harder to identify.

As discussed above initially cash-based businesses were one of the key areas on which money launderers would concentrate to launder their funds. Returning to the business of a launderette, this is an obvious example of such a suitable vehicle for the money launderer. Anyone can walk into a coin operated launderette and put their coins into the machine, or pay the attendant for laundry services. The payments will predominantly be in cash and there can be very little control to ensure that the funds that would be banked by the launderette business are actually the same as those that are received by the launderette. This therefore achieves the objectives of money laundering – the use of the launderette business will enable a criminal to disguise the source of their funds so that they appear to be from legitimate sources and can be freely used.

Clearly organised criminals are able to take advantage of any number of cash-based businesses to disguise illegal proceeds. The following are just a few of the types of business which have been subject to abuse by money launderers:

- launderettes
- newspaper sales
- taxis
- bars and fast food restaurants
- casinos
- insurance
- asset management
- antiques
- property.

Some of the vehicles will not be used for the primary placement of cash but will become part of the layering process are considered later in the chapter. Of course as detection of money laundering has become more sophisticated, then so has the use of the financial markets by the money launderer.

THE PROCESS OF MONEY LAUNDERING

Money laundering is essentially a three-stage process as discussed towards the end of this chapter. It starts with the criminal activity that gives rise to the illegal funds. We have mentioned the drug trafficking offences, but everything from tax evasion to bribery and corruption results in funds being produced which the criminal will seek to disguise. The funds need to first be received and then introduced into the system. It is often at this first introduction phase that the detection authorities have their best chance of identifying the funds, leading to criminal prosecution. This is followed by the layering and integration phases.

Clearly a series of fees and costs will need to be incurred by the launderer to achieve their object of disguising the original source of the funds. It is the combination of both the level of criminal activity in the world with the level of fees that may be earned that result in money laundering being such a lucrative industry. Of course as the money launderer becomes more sophisticated it is also incumbent on the financial intermediaries (banks, brokers, insurers, casinos and other entities) together with law enforcement agencies to also become more sophisticated and vigilant in their deliberations. This tends to result in new legislation being implemented to deal with what is the last problem that has been identified – whether it actually reduces money laundering is of course another matter. While we still have activities that we consider to be criminal we will have criminal proceeds and consequently money laundering to contend with.

THE PRIMARY OFFENCES

Initially the drive of the money laundering deterrence legislation was to restrict and identify the activities of organised criminals and gangs. This was then extended to the area of narcotics and drug trafficking, indeed much of the current legislation has drug trafficking prosecution at its heart. The idea is that by making it difficult for the syndicate that is producing the narcotics and then distributing them around the world to make use of the funds generated, there will be a reduction in the level of narcotics that is available and therefore drug taking will reduce.

In more recent years terrorist financing has also become a major cause for concern and again money laundering deterrence has been targeted as one of the ways in which the authorities within a country can be seen to be acting to attempt to reduce the ability of such organisations to act. So the three original key areas where money laundering deterrence legislation and regulation were intended to be effective were to reduce:

- organised crime
- drug trafficking
- terrorist financing.

All of these are clearly illegal activities in most countries, although they are not always easy to define completely or accurately. More recently in many countries the scope of such rules and regulations has significantly broadened, to become effectively what might be considered as all crimes legislation. This clearly results in a broadening of the areas of criminal activity being covered by such legislation, which would include some or all of the following:

- robbery or theft
- blackmail or extortion
- bribery and corruption
- piracy of various types
- illegal pornography or issues related to sexual matters

- people trafficking
- tax evasion.

DUE DILIGENCE

Whilst in the case of tax evasion the suspicion may not immediately be obvious, in other cases it will be. It is therefore important for financial institutions and other relevant entities to properly identify their customers and associates, undertaking what are referred to as due diligence procedures, or if they are high perceived risk, enhanced due diligence procedures.

Such procedures have as their objective the intention of identifying that the customer or associate is an appropriate person for the company to do business with. This will involve obtaining information on both people and companies and their source of funds.

After taking on the association the requirement to undertake due diligence does not end. The financial institution will still be required to undertake monitoring of the customer to see that the activities undertaken appear to be consistent with their understanding of the customer. This ongoing due diligence will continue throughout the customer relationship.

If a suspicion has been identified it does need to be investigated by the financial institution to ensure that there are real grounds for suspicion. Only then should the suspicion be reported to the relevant authorities by the relevant officer at the financial institution, a role normally referred to as that of the Money Laundering Reporting Officer (or MLRO). The suspicious activity report (or SAR) submitted to the relevant authority will potentially document that the financial institution has met their obligations under the relevant legislation, providing a safe harbour from prosecution.

THE EVASION OF TAXATION

There are few things more certain in life than taxation, unless you are lucky enough to be based in a jurisdiction where no taxes are in fact payable – certain countries in the Middle East, for example.

In most countries some or all of the following taxes apply:

- income tax
- corporation tax
- sales tax or Value Added Tax
- inheritance tax
- capital gains tax
- local sales tax
- car tax
- petroleum revenue tax
- gaming duty
- alcohol duties
- national insurance
- property taxes.

With such a range of possible taxes available that both individuals and businesses could suffer, it is hardly surprising that an industry has emerged to assist individuals and corporations to minimise the amount of taxation that they are required to pay.

When you are organising your affairs to minimise the taxation that would be levied, this is clearly a legal process. However, the failure to pay taxation that is due and payable is clearly a criminal offence and therefore would be covered by "all crime" money laundering deterrence rules and regulations. The problem is that taxation statutes and their legal interpretation are generally far from certain and therefore court action is often required to enable the legal position to be clarified with certainty.

To illustrate the problem, consider the following. A company is seeking to acquire another business. At the time when a transaction was entered into to buy the company the acquiring business may have thought that what they were doing was legal, and therefore that they were paying the correct sums of taxation to the relevant collecting authority. It may only be after the case has been resolved in favour of the taxation authorities that the firm would have been guilty of money laundering since they would have failed to pay the appropriate amount of taxation on the due date.

Of course in reality it is cases where there is a lack of clarity that tend to prove problematic and it is when the company is taking actions to minimise taxation which are perhaps pushing the boundaries that problems occur.

These problems have been well known for many years. There is of course nothing wrong in principle with tax shelters which are designed to enable executives to mitigate the impact of taxation.

This can be through reducing a rate of taxation or often more importantly to delay payment of taxation. Deferring income into a later period perhaps resulting in taxation being based on a remittance basis, or taking advantage of rules related to the taxation of stock options can all have major benefits. The accounting firms were keen to sell these products to their private clients and stock option schemes became prevalent. These schemes enabled executives to reduce their current taxation liabilities and also had a secondary advantage in that since the shares themselves would not be sold the price of the company's stock was also not impacted.

Challenging this type of scheme can be difficult and expensive for a tax authority. Even in the US penalties are limited and insufficient to deter the establishment of such schemes. A quotation from *USA Today* of 5 February 2003 stated that "There's so little fear right now of adverse consequences," says a congressional staff expert who asked to remain unnamed. "Penalties are fairly low, and even if you lose in court, you'll be paying back taxes at low interest rates."

So perhaps this has the effect of actually encouraging tax evasion and also of course money laundering.

SUSPICION AND REPORTING

The key issue is that actions taken by firms to attempt to reduce the level of their taxation may eventually be seen as being too extreme and therefore could potentially be considered to be illegal. If a country adopts an all crime approach to money laundering deterrence then there may be a requirement for such matters to immediately be reported to the reporting authorities, since immediately there is a suspicion. Of course the point at which the suspicion occurs may be unclear.

A suspicious activity report (or SAR) will typically then be provided to the relevant in-country authority for them to consider whether action should be taken. In many cases the authorities will not have sufficient information to take action, in which case nothing will happen. In other cases they will link information from the single SAR with other SARs that they receive, leading to information linking investigations and ultimately to criminal prosecution.

THE LOCAL SERVICE PROVIDER

Do you have any local service providers that you pay in cash? This would include plumbers, carpenters, gardeners, taxi drivers, builders and similar parties. Would you expect that person to disclose all of their income to the relevant taxation authorities? Is it possible that they may choose to show a lower amount of revenue than is actually the case to reduce the amount of taxation that would be due and payable? This is clearly a plausible scenario, but is it sufficient to result in the money laundering deterrence regime applying and a SAR being produced?

Generally such activities are to some extent not included within this form of legislation. Basically it would not be helpful for financial institutions and others to report cash-based businesses to the relevant authorities purely because they were cash-based businesses. Just because it is possible for the activity to permit tax evasion, does not mean that there actually will be tax evasion and therefore generally this cannot be sufficient to result in a suspicion of money laundering and consequent reporting to the approved party. However if there was a clear suspicion then such reporting should still take place.

Could there also be obligations on a financial institution regarding the under-reporting of income or some other form of tax evasion? The answer is clearly yes. If the firm should have been aware that the firm was under reporting its income or in some other way evading taxation unlawfully then this would be a reason to report the firm to the relevant authorities and for the money laundering deterrence legislation to apply.

LICENCE PAYMENTS

In some countries it will be illegal to drive without a driving licence, or to operate a specific car without the vehicle having been approved, or to have a television without a relevant approval. Such areas are generally seen as being too minor to warrant investigation by relevant authorities and are therefore generally seen as more minor offences. Accordingly retaining the funds that you should have paid for the licence will not in itself mean that you are guilty of money laundering offences in addition to the offence resulting from failure to have the licence.

What this means is that as you move from one jurisdiction to another it is always important to make sure that you are fully aware of what are the predicate offences within the specific jurisdiction that you are involved with. It is also important to stress that some jurisdictions include an element of extraterritorial provisions, enabling the regulator in one country to take an interest in payments in another country, with the USA being one obvious such case as set out in Chapter 7.

Of course tax evasion is not at the heart of the money laundering deterrence regime, yet it is increasingly one of the major areas where such legislation is applied. Understanding the local regulatory requirements for due diligence, monitoring and reporting, training staff adequately and rigorously applying relevant procedures is always the best protection for any firm in any jurisdiction.

THE PROCESS OF MONEY LAUNDERING

The money laundering cycle

Money laundering is generally seen as a three stage process.

Stage 1: Placement
Stage 2: Layering
Stage 3: Integration

The idea is that the initial proceeds enter the banking system at a perceived point of weakness and then the funds are moved around such that the initial source of the funds is disguised. The funds are eventually reintegrated into the mainstream banking system as clean funds.

These three stages will be considered separately.

The placement phase

The placement is the initial stage of the process. The illegitimate funds have been obtained in some way, perhaps as a result of theft or drug trafficking. These funds will need to be initially placed into the banking system to start the money laundering process.

Placement is not just the movement of cash into a bank account, even though this is the process that is most frequently considered.

The initial placement purely means moving the funds from their original cash source into some other form which will enable the money launderer to undertake further layering and therefore disguise these amounts.

For example, were a money launderer to purchase a physical asset, say a painting or another asset of value, then this asset could be subsequently sold and this would then release funds which would appear to be legitimate. So it is not just the placement of cash into a bank account that represents the first stage in the layering process, rather it is the initial transfer of assets into another form.

Money launderers will typically focus on areas where there is the least obvious control. Consequently, if the money launderer has particular knowledge that an individual or company is in particular need of cash, then this will probably be the opportunity that is selected for the original placement of illegitimate funds.

All of the following could be used for the placement process:

- the purchase of paintings
- the purchase of antiques
- buying things in a market
- the acquisition of stamps and coins
- the purchase of investment products
- taking out unnecessary insurance products
- the purchase of new or second hand cars
- the purchase of boats
- buying chips at a casino
- purchasing lottery tickets
- purchasing premium bonds
- acquiring shares in private companies
- providing cash loans to companies
- purchasing commodities or precious metals.

Effectively the placement is purely limited by the vision of the money launderer.

If there is a branch of a bank that is known to be under pressure to increase their deposit base, then the money launderers will actively seek them out. If there is a bank that is struggling to maintain liquidity then they may also become an obvious target. If a salesman is given a target to achieve a bonus then they may also become an opportunity for the money launderer since they will be potentially liable to lower their money laundering deterrence guard while they are seeking to achieve sales. It is the person or business that most needs the cash or sales that is most likely to be targeted by the unscrupulous.

The layering phase

Once the funds have initially been placed the next phase is the layering phase. As stated above the objective of the layering phase is to disguise the proceeds such that the original source and the current position of the funds are unclear. This can typically be as easy as simply using the illegitimate funds to invest in something legitimate, so that the funds now appear to be "clean". In other cases a far more complex series of transactions will be entered into.

In more complex schemes, the money launderer will move the funds between a number of accounts in a number of different jurisdictions and through a series of companies to ensure that the trail is as complicated as is possible. This will essentially obscure the audit trail and sever the link with the original criminal proceeds. In the most professional cases of money laundering identified, the funds can actually "spin" up to ten times prior to being integrated into the banking system.

Money launderers will face varying levels of difficulty during the layering stage depending on the chosen method of investment. For example antiques, paintings and stamps can all be legitimately acquired privately, and thus have a low level of risk for the money launderer. You can purchase them at antique markets, shops, auctions or even car boot sales or flea markets. They can be inherited, found or gifted. Some of these routes maintain formal records of the purchase or sale, whereas others do not. If no questions are asked, then the money launderer is clearly at a significant advantage. A more risky method of layering would be the purchase of property as lawyers may become involved, who may be alerted to concerns as a result of their own due diligence, which will be carried out when larger transfers of money are made. They may also be under an obligation to report inappropriate activity.

The integration phase

Integration is the final stage of the money laundering process. It is the stage where illegal proceeds are re-integrated into a legitimate financial system to be assimilated with other assets in the system. This is where the disguised criminal proceeds can be returned to and used by the money launderer and they will now appear to be legitimate funds. Money launderers will typically put the "cleaned" money into the normal economy to make it appear to have been legitimately earned. The main aim of the money launderer is to successfully integrate funds so that it becomes difficult for anyone to distinguish between legitimate and illegitimate (criminal proceeds) funds and they will then be free to use them for any purpose they require.

There are many ways in which laundered money can be integrated back into the normal economy. With the money launderer, however, the main objective of money laundering at this stage is to reunite themselves with the criminal proceeds in a manner that does not draw attention or suspicion. More about suspicion later, but it is often by the money launderer abusing successful schemes of money laundering through greed that the financial institution subsequently becomes suspicious and the criminal identified.

For example, the purchases of property, sports cars, art work, jewellery etc. are common ways for the launderer to enjoy their laundered money without necessarily drawing attention to them. The risk is that conspicuous displays of wealth could either cause suspicion or result in envy leading to identification of inappropriate actions. However, money launderers will use more and more creative and unique ways to achieve their objectives.

Common methods of integration used by money launderers include the following:

- The simplest method of integrating funds is to transfer money to a legitimate bank from a shell bank owned by the launderers.
- Money launderers can send embellished invoices overvaluing goods or services which allow them to move funds from one country to another. The invoices act as verification for the origins of the funds placed with financial institutions.
- Money launderers can establish anonymous companies in countries where the right to secrecy is guaranteed. They are then able to grant themselves loans out of the laundered money in the event of a future legal transaction. Furthermore, they may increase their profits; they will also claim tax relief on the loan repayments and charge themselves interest on the loan.
- The money launderer can cancel an insurance policy after the premium has been paid. The return of the premium by the insurance company is of course laundered funds.

- Assets acquired can be sold either in an open market or as a private sale with funds being received ideally electronically into a legitimate bank account, perfectly laundered of course.

These are but a few of the ways in which the assets can be integrated back into the normal economy. Their objective is normally to obtain cash payment from a legitimate bank that they can pay into their account at another legitimate bank. Once this has been achieved the laundering cycle is normally complete and the criminal is free to use the funds for any purpose they require.

Chapter 2

INTERNATIONAL MONEY LAUNDERING REGULATION – THE ROLE OF THE FINANCIAL ACTION TASK FORCE

WHO ARE THE FINANCIAL ACTION TASK FORCE?

The Financial Action Task Force (FATF) is an inter-governmental body created in 1989 to encourage policies to protect the global financial system against money laundering. The FATF operates as a policy-making body, using its political strength to bring about national and international regulatory and legislative change. The staff of the FATF assess the international money laundering deterrence policies which are locally in place on a country by country basis against their issued guidelines. They issue formal reports and make recommendations addressed to the relevant reporting or responsible body of each country relating to the implementation of their individual policy framework.

The FATF assesses a country's policy framework with reference to the international standards that it has issued in respect of the anti-money laundering measures it expects a country to have implemented. These measures consist of 40 Recommendations together with an additional nine Special Recommendations. Both sets of recommendations need to be implemented by countries on a national level in order to be legally binding since the FATF itself does not have any enforcement capability other than putting a particular country onto a list of noncompliant countries.

It must be emphasised that the risk that this could impose upon a country is severe since it will negatively impact the ability of any country to undertake international cross-border business due to the additional controls and due diligence procedures which would be likely to have been applied against them.

History of FATF

The FATF was established as a result of the G7 Summit held in Paris in 1989. The Heads of State Governments, Presidents from the G7 member states and the European Commission formed the initial Task Force. The Task Force's main objective was to examine existing money laundering techniques and trends on both national and international levels, making recommendations for their improvement as appropriate. This then enabled the Task Force to establish which specific measures still needed to be developed and implemented.

The FATF has since established its 40 Recommendations detailing a comprehensive plan of action to fight against money laundering. An additional nine Special Recommendations were introduced as a response to the September 11 2001 terrorist attacks in America. These additional Special Recommendations set out the basic framework to detect, prevent and suppress the financing of terrorism and terrorist acts. Again these need to be implemented into local legislation or regulation since the FATF does not have any global direct regulatory responsibility.

The 40 FATF Recommendations

The 40 Recommendations were first introduced in 1990 and aim to act as countermeasures against international money laundering. Countries are given a degree of flexibility within their own constitutional frameworks regarding their implementation as the Recommendations do not constitute a legally binding international convention. However, the Recommendations have been endorsed by numerous international bodies and all major countries are united by a political commitment to combating money laundering and complying with these Regulations.

The 40 Recommendations were last revised in 2003, and are summarised below.

Recommendation 1

- Countries should criminalise money laundering on the basis of the United Nations Vienna and Palermo Conventions.
- Countries should apply the crime of money laundering to all offences, to include the widest range of predicate offences.
- Predicate offences for money laundering should extend to conduct that occurred in another country, which constitutes an offence in that country, and which would have constituted a predicate offence had it occurred domestically. Countries may provide that the only prerequisite is that the conduct would have constituted a predicate offence had it occurred domestically.
- Countries may provide that the offence of money laundering does not apply to persons who committed the predicate offence, where this is required by fundamental principles of their domestic law.

The key issue here is that money laundering is not purely related to drug trafficking and financial crime, but the intention of the Regulations is that it becomes an all crime offence. This idea of "all crime" starts to be an area where there are differences between local implementations of the Recommendations. One specific area is tax evasion – remember tax avoidance is legal, but tax evasion is illegal. If it is illegal then movements of proceeds of cash related to the predicate offence of tax evasion will become money laundering and action will need to be taken.

The definition of what constitutes criminal activity the proceeds of which become money laundering does vary considerably between countries, so there is always a requirement to ensure that the predicate offence is actually caught by the local jurisdiction's implementation of the Regulations.

There is a problem with predicate offences that cross national borders. Bull fighting is illegal in the United Kingdom, but not in Spain, for example. Does this mean that a UK bank could never become involved with a firm that earns funds from bullfighting? Does that mean that legitimate funds could become illegitimate if they cross boundaries? Actually this is generally not the case and some degree of common sense may be applied – but remember that common sense is not really very common.

Recommendation 2

- Countries should ensure that the intent and knowledge required to prove the offence of money laundering is consistent with the Vienna and Palermo Conventions and based on objective factual circumstances.
- Countries should ensure that criminal liability, and where that is not possible civil and administrative liability, should apply to legal persons. This should not preclude parallel proceedings with respect to legal persons in countries where such forms of liability are available. Legal persons should be subject to effective, dissuasive and proportionate sanctions and these measures should be without prejudice to the criminal liability of individuals.

This is the first time that the idea of suspicion is actually addressed. The recommendation requires factual circumstances to prove money laundering, so rumour is clearly insufficient. Each country does implement slightly different rules regarding what is a suspicion that should be reported to the relevant authorities and what is a rumour that may essentially be ignored. We go into this issue further in later chapters of this book.

Notice there is a requirement for sanctions to be proportionate, so the ability to pay is generally taken into account in deciding upon relevant sanctions.

Recommendation 3

- Countries should adopt legislative measures to enable their competent authorities to confiscate property laundered and proceeds from money laundering or predicate offences, without prejudice to bone fide third parties.
- Measures should include the authority to
  (a) identify, trace and evaluate property subject to confiscation;
  (b) freeze, seize and dispose of property;
  (c) void any actions which prevent the state's ability to confiscate property;
  (d) take any appropriate investigative measures.

This recommendation requires the competent authorities to seize the assets of money launderers. Of course there is normally different legislation regarding such matters which normally covers all crime, not just money laundering. For example direct theft of an asset (e.g. a car) would already be typically caught by such legislation. What this recommendation achieves is to extend this to all areas of money laundering. It tends to result in physical property and bank accounts being seized, as well as high profile cars.

Recommendation 4

- A country's financial institutions' secrecy laws should not inhibit the implementation of FATF.

This is perhaps one of the more contentious recommendations. Clearly offshore and other financial centres have for many years taken advantage of data secrecy regulations to prevent disclosure of confidential information to enquiring regulatory agents. This Recommendation sought to reduce the incidence of such approaches and more recent political pressures have resulted in greater relaxation of such secrecy rules in money laundering or tax evasion enquiries.

Its application has been fraught with some disclosures by financial institutions in certain countries actually being challenged by the courts and being found to be illegal. The offshore centres market their secrecy credentials to attract the business that they are seeking. This requirement begins to put all of this potentially at risk.

Recommendation 5

- Financial institutions should not keep anonymous accounts.
- Financial institutions should undertake Customer care Due Diligence (CDD) measures which include identifying and verifying their customers in a variety of circumstances. The following CDD measures should be undertaken:
  (a) identifying and verifying the customer's identity using reliable independent data and information;
  (b) taking steps to identify the beneficial owner of an account;
  (c) obtaining information on the purpose and nature of the business relationship;
  (d) conducting ongoing due diligence on the business relationship and undertaking and maintaining appropriate scrutiny of transactions throughout the course of that relationship.

This recommendation tries to get to the heart of money laundering deterrence processes and procedures. The customer needs to be properly identified and monitored throughout the business relationship with the financial institution. Further the ultimate beneficial owner needs to be identified and anonymous accounts are to be prohibited. In the past banks maintained numbered accounts to protect the identity of customers – such a practice is effectively no longer appropriate. In all such cases the bank will be required to record and identify the actual beneficial owner of the account.

Recommendation 6

- Financial institutions should carry out additional due diligence measures in relation to politically exposed persons by:
  (a) having risk management systems to determine whether a customer is a politically exposed person;
  (b) obtaining senior management approval when dealing with such customers;
  (c) taking reasonable measures to establish the source of wealth and funds;
  (d) Conducting enhanced monitoring of the business.

Politically exposed persons clearly provide a higher level of risk for a financial institution. Of course the key question is who is a politically exposed person (or a PEP) and what actual additional steps should be conducted. This is addressed further in Chapter 14.

Recommendation 7

- Financial institutions should carry out extra due diligence regarding cross-border correspondent banking business by taking the following measures:
  - (a) gathering sufficient information about a correspondent institution in order to understand their nature and reputation, including whether it has previously been subject to investigations or regulatory action;
  - (b) assessing correspondent banking institutions' anti-money laundering and terrorist financing controls;
  - (c) obtaining management approval for new correspondent relationships;
  - (d) documenting the responsibilities of each institution with regard to identification and monitoring of customer accounts;
  - (e) undertaking ongoing due diligence with respect to "payable-through accounts" with direct access to the accounts of the correspondent.

What is important about this Recommendation is that it clearly states that one financial institution cannot just rely on work conducted by another financial institution. Indeed some regulators have taken this to the extent that a holding company bank cannot rely on work conducted by one of its overseas subsidiaries without undertaking additional work. Clearly a series of set procedures would need to be implemented by any financial institution to comply with what could actually be quite onerous requirements and one would also expect a bank to have a standard response available when asked about the nature of the policies and procedures adopted locally to prevent or detect money laundering.

Recommendation 8

- Financial institutions should pay special attention to money laundering threats relating to technologies which might favour anonymity.

- Financial institutions should have procedures in place to reduce the additional risks associated with undertaking non face-to-face business.

This Recommendation deals with two potentially high risk areas. Many new technologies result in the customer being even more remote from the financial institution undertaking the transfer. This could result in the financial institution having less personal knowledge of the customer than would previously have been the case. The use of the internet, for example, could be one such mechanism. If the financial institution is not likely to arrange for one of its employees to actually meet the client then they do face the issue that recognising the customer from a picture is almost impossible. Consequently personal identification is harder. It may also be harder to get information about the customer that can be independently verified.

All the Recommendation requires is that such circumstances are identified and that additional procedures are implemented to deal effectively with this threat. These procedures are generally referred to as enhanced due diligence and are those additional procedures which the financial institution considers appropriate in the circumstances.

Recommendation 9

- Countries may permit financial institutions to instruct third parties to perform elements (a)–(c) of the Cross Border Due Diligence process (Recommendation 7), provided that the criteria set out below are met. However ultimate responsibility for customer identification will remain with the financial institution.
- The criteria that should be met are as follows:
  - (a) A financial institution should immediately obtain the necessary information concerning elements (a)–(c) of the CDD process.
  - (b) They must also satisfy themselves that copies of identification data and other documentation relating to the CDD requirements will be made available from the third party upon request without delay.
  - (c) The financial institution should satisfy itself that the third party is regulated and supervised, and has measures in place to comply with the CDD requirements in line with Recommendations 5 and 10.

Third parties instructed by financial institutions to perform cross-border Due Diligence may be based in other countries. However, institutions must pay particular attention to countries which do not adequately apply the FATF Recommendations.

This Recommendation actually provides more clarification to previous recommendations. The focus on the regulations in the country is important and therefore financial institutions need to know which are considered as noncooperative countries. Of course most financial institutions will also grade countries using their own internal information and such analysis will drive the level of analysis that they will conduct. You would expect financial institutions to err on the side of caution and, if possible, conduct procedures that are adequate to enable the board to have the confidence that they require. Such procedures as a financial institution actually conducts are likely to greatly exceed these minimum requirements.

Recommendation 10

- Financial institutions should maintain records of transactions for up to five years, in order to assist competent authorities with information requests.
- Records must be sufficient to permit reconstruction of individual transactions and to provide enough evidence for criminal prosecution.
- Identification data obtained through the customer due diligence process must also be retained for at least five years after the business relationship is ended.
- The identification data and transaction records should be available to domestic competent authorities upon appropriate authority.

Again it must be recognised that these are minimum requirements for the assessment of the money laundering deterrence procedures adopted at a country level. The important issue here is the requirement to maintain due diligence records for five years after the end of a relationship with a client. It is incumbent on financial institutions to ensure that their document retention (or destruction) policies are consistent with this objective. Indeed such a policy would be sensible with or without such a recommendation since such records are often required when a case ends up in some form of legal dispute and it is the original records from the time of sale which become crucial evidence.

Recommendation 11

- Special attention should be drawn to all complex, unusual, large transactions, and unusual patterns of transactions, which have no apparent economic or visible lawful purpose.
- The background and purpose of such transactions should be examined and made available to help competent authorities and auditors.

This is the first recommendation which is starting to look at monitoring and patterns of behaviour. The objective is for the financial institution to identify transactions which would not appear to be consistent with their understanding of the nature, history and understanding of their client. While these seem like easy requirements to state, this is not easy to actually undertake in practice and may require relatively complex software to achieve it. In the absence of such solutions being implemented (see Chapter 23), the management rely on their personal knowledge and ability to see such transactions.

The question then is what needs to be done in such circumstances and what records are to be maintained. As we shall see this is dealt with in later recommendations.

Recommendation 12

- The customer due diligence and record-keeping requirements set out in Recommendations 5, 6, and 8 to 11 should apply to designated nonfinancial businesses and professions in the following situations:
    - (a) Casinos – which involve financial transactions equal to or above the applicable designated threshold.
    - (b) Real estate agents – for client transactions concerning the buying and selling of real estate.
    - (c) Dealers in precious metals and dealers in precious stones – for transactions with customers equal to or above the applicable designated threshold.
    - (d) Lawyers, notaries, other independent legal professionals and accountants when they prepare for or carry out transactions for their client concerning the following activities:
        - buying and selling of real estate;
        - managing of client money, securities or other assets;
        - management of bank, savings or securities accounts;
        - organisation of contributions for the creation, operation or management of companies;

 - ○ creation, operation or management of legal persons or arrangements, and buying and selling of business entities.

(e) Trust and company service providers when they prepare for or carry out transactions for a client concerning the activities listed in the definition in the Glossary included within the FATF Guidance.

This composite recommendation seeks to broaden the money laundering requirements beyond the financial services sector, picking up accountants, lawyers, casinos, estate agents and trust providers, amongst others. This then leads to an interesting issue as who within the relevant jurisdiction actually takes ownership of the regulation in such areas. Sometimes it is obvious, as may be the case for chartered accountancy or legal practices – whereas in others they may actually be unregulated. Are casinos and real estate agents regulated in all countries? Accordingly it will be important for the financial institution to verify the legal regulatory structure that is in place in all such cases.

Recommendation 13

- If a financial institution suspects that funds are the proceeds of a criminal activity, or are related to terrorist financing, it should be required by law or regulation to report its suspicions to the financial intelligence unit (FIU).

Different jurisdictions actually have different reporting requirements, so for an international bank this can be a significant operational issue. The importance of reporting is that it generally provides the reporting entity with some form of protection from being engaged in money laundering, although there is normally also a requirement for investigation to be conducted to ensure that the reporting actually does not provide the FIU with a level of information that would inhibit their ability to function effectively.

Recommendation 14

- Financial institutions, their directors, officers and employees should be:

  (a) protected by legal provisions from criminal and civil liability if they report their suspicions in good faith to the FIU, even if they did not know whether illegal activity actually occurred;

(b) prohibited by law from disclosing the fact that a suspicious transaction or related information is being reported to the FIU.

Paragraph (a) provides the protection that the officers require. Of course (b) could become a problem were allegations made against a firm that had actually reported their suspicion. They are in the position where they are unable to respond to allegations and newspaper stories without breaching legal provisions and this can result in unfortunate consequences.

It is important for information services, such as newspapers and Reuters, to appreciate this issue and consider the implications when they are making allegations.

Recommendation 15

- Financial institutions should develop programmes against money laundering and terrorist financing.
- These programmes should include:
  (a) developing internal policies, procedures and controls, including appropriate compliance management arrangements, and adequate screening procedures to ensure high standards when hiring employees;
  (b) an ongoing employee training programme;
  (c) an audit function to test the system.

While this is placing clear obligations on financial institutions, the reference to internal audit at this stage is important. Whether the internal audit function actually includes the testing of the anti-money laundering procedures, policies, controls and training within its scope is an issue which financial institutions should address. To meet these obligations you would expect that such functions should exist, fully address the area and be adequately staffed and trained.

Recommendation 16

- The requirements set out in Recommendations 13 to 15, and 21 apply to all designated nonfinancial businesses and professions, subject to the following qualifications:
  (a) Lawyers, notaries, other independent legal professionals and accountants should be required to report suspicious transactions when they engage in a financial transaction in relation to the activities described in Recommendation

12(d). Reporting requirements are strongly recommended to extend to the professional activities of accountants, including auditing.

(b) Dealers in precious metals and dealers in precious stones should report suspicious cash transactions equal to or above the applicable designated threshold.

(c) Trust and company service providers should report suspicious transactions for a client when, on behalf of or for a client, they engage in a transaction in relation to the activities referred to in Recommendation 12(e).

- Lawyers, notaries, other independent legal professionals and accountants acting as independent legal professionals, are not required to report their suspicions if information obtained is subject to professional secrecy or legal professional privilege.

This provides clarification to Recommendation 12. Notice that legal privilege is enshrined in the Regulations. This is to prevent a lawyer needing to report all of their clients that could be potentially guilty of a predicate offence to the relevant authorities. This would run contrarily to the objectives of a natural justice judicial system since it would reduce openness between a client and their legal advisor. Accordingly the recommendation to maintain legal privilege appears sensible.

The company service provider rules vary enormously between jurisdictions. It is primarily aimed at firms that create offshore companies and provide them with services. It does in principle also capture administrators and other service providers – yet in many countries there is no body that is in a position to effectively regulate the implementation of such rules.

Recommendation 17

- Countries should ensure that effective, proportionate and dissuasive sanctions are in place to deal with persons covered by these Recommendations who fail to comply with anti-money laundering or terrorist financing requirements.

The idea that the sanction should be such as to dissuade someone from undertaking money laundering is interesting. Whether they are actually effective given the number of prosecutions in a relevant jurisdiction is something that needs to be considered. I am not sure that any criminal would actually be dissuaded from undertaking criminal activity by the imposition of money laundering deterrence regimes.

Recommendation 18

- Financial institutions should refuse to enter into, or continue, a correspondent banking relationship with shell banks.
- This also extends to respondent foreign financial institutions that permit their accounts to be used by shell banks.

A shell bank is really a fake. It appears to be a bank but has no real business and is therefore a conduit for money laundering. Consequently a financial institution must make sure that they have a real understanding of the activity of the financial institution that they are entering into a business relationship with. As you can clearly see, the FATF expects due diligence to extend to financial institutions.

Recommendation 19

- Countries should consider the utility of implementing a system of placing central national agencies, where financial institutions can report international currency transactions above a certain threshold. This would then enable competent authorities to access a computerised database in money laundering or terrorist financing cases.

Such systems have now been implemented in most jurisdictions with varying levels of success. In some cases the length of time between making a report and receiving a response from the relevant authority is such as to undermine the efficacy of the process – whereas others are successful in providing adequate and timely information. The level of threshold that may be implemented may vary and in some countries to identify low payment style money laundering a nil threshold is applied. The type of activity that may be identified by linked small payments might be illegal pornography, for example.

Recommendation 20

- Countries should consider applying the FATF Recommendations to any business or profession that poses a money laundering or terrorist financing risk.
- Countries should further encourage the development of modern and secure techniques of money management that are less vulnerable to money laundering.

This is a hopeful recommendation looking for a change in society without any real ability to influence such change.

Recommendation 21

- Financial institutions should give special attention to transactions with countries which do not, or insufficiently, apply the FATF Recommendations.
- Where these transactions have no apparent economic or visible lawful purpose, their background and purpose should be examined and made available to help competent authorities.
- Where such a country continues not to apply, or insufficiently applies, the FATF Recommendations, countries should be able to apply appropriate countermeasures.

This requires the higher level of due diligence (or enhanced due diligence) to be conducted in the case of what are termed noncooperative countries. Such information is available on the FATF web site.

Recommendation 22

- Recommendation 21 should also extend to branches and majority owned subsidiaries located abroad, especially in countries which do not apply, or have insufficiently applied, the FATF Recommendations, to the extent that local applicable laws and regulations permit.
- When local applicable laws and regulations prohibit this implementation, competent authorities in the country of the parent institution should be informed by the financial institutions that they cannot apply the FATF Recommendations.

The important issue here is the branch issue. Recognise that a branch is normally not a legal entity. What it means is that a financial institution needs to take notice of the booking location rather than just the contracting location in determining the level of due diligence that is to be conducted.

Recommendation 23

- Countries implementing the FATF Recommendations should be subject to adequate regulation and supervision.
- Competent authorities should take the necessary legal measures to prevent criminals becoming the beneficial owner of a

significant or controlling interest or holding a management function in a financial institution.

- Financial institutions should ensure regulatory and supervisory measures that apply for prudential purposes are also relevant to money laundering and terrorist financing deterrence purposes.
- Other financial institutions should also be licensed, registered, regulated and subject to supervision or oversight for anti-money laundering purposes, having regard to the risk of money laundering or terrorist financing in that sector.
- Businesses providing a service of money or value transfer, or of money or currency changing should be licensed or registered, and subject to effective systems for monitoring and ensuring compliance with national requirements to combat money laundering and terrorist financing.

This Recommendation brings money exchange businesses into the general jurisdiction of money laundering deterrence legislation, although whether such a transfer vehicle is monitored as well as registered is an issue which needs to be considered. The obligation on controllers not being money launderers is a requirement placed on the competent authorities, but is not easy to implement in practice in many jurisdictions. The money launderer will hide behind another party who may appear to be legitimate enabling them to conduct their activities.

Recommendation 24

- Designated nonfinancial businesses and professions should be subject to regulatory and supervisory measures as set out below.
  - (a) Casinos should be subject to a regime that ensures that they have effectively implemented the necessary anti-money laundering and terrorist financing measures. At a minimum:
    - ○ casinos should be licensed;
    - ○ competent authorities should take the necessary legal or regulatory measures to prevent criminals or their associates from holding or being the beneficial owner of a significant or controlling interest, holding a management function in, or being an operator of a casino;
    - ○ competent authorities should ensure that casinos are effectively supervised for compliance with requirements to combat money laundering and terrorist financing.
  - (b) Countries should ensure that the other categories of designated nonfinancial businesses and professions are subject to

effective systems and requirements to combat money laundering and terrorist financing. This should be performed on a risk-sensitive basis by a government authority or by an appropriate self-regulatory organisation, provided that such an organisation can ensure that its members comply with their obligations to combat money laundering and terrorist financing.

Again this Recommendation is really only providing clarification to other existing Recommendations.

Recommendation 25

- The competent authorities should establish guidelines, and provide feedback which will assist financial institutions and designated nonfinancial businesses and professions in applying national measures to combat money laundering and terrorist financing, and in particular, in detecting and reporting suspicious transactions.

Of course in designing such guidelines some authorities will add additional requirements of which the international bank must be aware. Clearly different authorities respond in differing ways with varying levels of information, but at least this Recommendation sets the objective clearly. In some countries by the time a response is received from the regulatory agency the money launderer will have been long gone, effectively undermining the entire process.

Recommendation 26

- Countries should establish a Financial Intelligence Unit (or FIU) that serves as a national centre for the receiving and analysis of suspicious transaction or activity reports (STRs or SARs) and other information regarding potential money laundering or terrorist financing.
- The FIU should have access, directly or indirectly, on a timely basis to the financial, administrative and law enforcement information that it requires to properly undertake its functions, including the analysis of SARs.

This is the central body that maintains all of the information which is intended to enable them to add information from different sources to build a picture of actual money laundering or terrorist financing requiring additional investigation – leading to prosecution.

It may well be that different suspicion reports from different financial institutions in combination may provide a larger picture of the problems encountered than is the case in the single report. This enables the FIU to see the whole environment in which the potentially inappropriate individual or operation is acting and obtain such additional information as they require for their purposes leading to regulatory or legal action being taken.

Recommendation 27

- Countries should ensure that designated law enforcement authorities have responsibility for money laundering and terrorist financing investigations.
- Countries are encouraged to support and develop special investigative techniques suitable for the investigation of money laundering.
- Countries are also encouraged to use other permanent or temporary groups specialised in asset investigation, and cooperative investigations with appropriate competent authorities in other countries.

This recommendation places obligations on law enforcement agencies to act effectively and proactively.

Recommendation 28

- Competent authorities should be able to obtain documents and information for use in those investigations, and in prosecutions when conducting investigations of money laundering.
- This should include powers to use compulsory measures for the production of records held by financial institutions and other persons and for the seizure and obtaining of evidence.

The issue with this recommendation and indeed with much money laundering deterrence legislation is how it interacts with other legal rights and regulations, whether statutory or guidance, issued in the relevant jurisdiction. This Recommendation really asks individual countries to deal with the complexity of their regulatory and legal framework to facilitate the investigation that is required.

Recomendation 29

- Supervisors should have adequate powers to monitor and ensure compliance by financial institutions with rules and regulations

implemented locally to combat money laundering and terrorist financing, including the authority to conduct inspections.
- They should be authorised to compel production of any information that is relevant to monitoring such compliance, and to impose adequate administrative sanctions for failure to comply with such requirements.

Again this Recommendation is concerned with the legal framework and investigative powers of the relevant authority, seeking to ensure that they have sufficient powers to enable them to meet their obligations.

Recommendation 30

- Countries should provide their competent authorities with adequate financial, human and technical resources.
- Countries should have processes to ensure that the staff of those authorities are of high integrity.

This Recommendation is effectively asking one group of money laundering deterrence people to require the appointment of even more money laundering deterrence people. A case of work for colleagues, perhaps?

Recommendation 31

- Countries should ensure that policy makers, the FIU, law enforcement and supervisors are able to cooperate, and where appropriate coordinate domestically with each other concerning the development and implementation of policies and activities to combat money laundering and terrorist financing.

The Recommendation is recognising the split responsibilities that may exist in many jurisdictions and to consider and mitigate the impact that this could make on effective money laundering deterrence in the absence of clear coordination.

Recommendation 32

- Countries should ensure that their competent authorities can review the effectiveness of their systems to combat money laundering and terrorist financing systems by maintaining comprehensive statistics on matters relevant to the effectiveness and efficiency of such systems.

One would hope that the competent authorities review effectiveness by more than looking at statistics, but at least this Recommendation requires that statistics are maintained. This means of course statistics on identified and reported money laundering and terrorist financing – not the actual population much of which will not have been identified.

Recommendation 33

- Countries should take measures to prevent the unlawful use of legal persons by money launderers.
- In particular, countries that have legal persons that are able to issue bearer shares should take appropriate adequate measures to ensure they are not misused for money laundering.
- Countries could consider measures to facilitate access to beneficial ownership and control information to financial institutions undertaking the requirements set out in Recommendation 5.

The issue with bearer instruments is that the issuing financial institution or body does not know who is actually holding the instrument and that when the instrument is cashed it is not possible to prove that the holder of the instrument is the beneficial owner. Consequently bearer instruments are ideal for money laundering, and therefore you have this Recommendation.

You would expect a financial institution to be alert to the additional risks that bearer documents present to them and to have specific additional procedures to attempt to confirm that the holder has not, for example, stolen the paper.

Recommendation 34

- Countries should take measures to prevent the unlawful use of legal arrangements by money launderers.
- In particular, countries should ensure that there is adequate, accurate and timely information on express trusts, including information on the settlor, trustee and beneficiaries, which can be obtained or accessed in a timely fashion by competent authorities.
- Countries could consider measures to facilitate access to beneficial ownership and control information by financial institutions undertaking the requirements as set out in Recommendation 5.

The trust issue has already been referred to. There is a concern that trusts can be used as vehicles for money laundering and, when you recall that tax evasion and avoidance of exchange control regulation are already predicate offences, then the issue becomes clearer. What FATF are seeking here is for information on such trusts to be maintained to enable additional data to be obtained to support other investigations.

Recommendation 35

- Countries should take immediate steps to become party to and implement fully the Vienna Convention, the Palermo Convention, and the 1999 United Nations International Convention for the Suppression of the Financing of Terrorism. Countries are also encouraged to ratify and implement other relevant international conventions, such as the 1990 Council of Europe Convention on Laundering, Search, Seizure and Confiscation of the Proceeds from Crime and the 2002 Inter-American Convention against Terrorism.

Most of which we have already really addressed in the first 34 Recommendations!

Recommendation 36

- Countries should provide the widest possible range of mutual legal assistance in relation to money laundering and terrorist financing investigations, prosecutions, and related proceedings. In particular, countries should:
  (a) not prohibit or place unreasonable or unduly restrictive conditions on the provision of mutual legal assistance;
  (b) ensure that they have clear and efficient processes for the execution of mutual legal assistance requests;
  (c) not refuse to execute a request for mutual legal assistance on the sole ground that the offence is also considered to involve fiscal matters;
  (d) not refuse to execute a request for mutual legal assistance on the grounds that laws require financial institutions to maintain secrecy or confidentiality.
- Countries should ensure that the powers of their competent authorities required under Recommendation 28 are also available for use in response to requests for mutual legal assistance, and if consistent with their domestic framework, in response to

direct requests from foreign judicial or law enforcement authorities to domestic counterparts.

- To avoid conflicts of jurisdiction mechanisms should exist to determine the best venue for prosecution of defendants in the interests of justice.

Recommendation 36 is really all about international cooperation. Major rings of money laundering will cover multiple jurisdictions and accordingly one regulator alone will not have the complete picture. International cooperation facilitates the effective information exchange necessary to properly understand the international web of transactions which would underpin a major money laundering investigation.

Recommendation 37

- Countries should, to the greatest extent possible, render mutual legal assistance notwithstanding the absence of dual criminality.
- Where dual criminality is required for mutual legal assistance or extradition, that requirement should be deemed to be satisfied regardless of whether both countries place the offence within the same category of offence or denominate the offence by the same terminology, provided that both countries criminalise the conduct underlying the offence.

This recommendation is worded to avoid the double jeopardy problem where one party could potentially be prosecuted in more than one place for the same offence. It also tries to deal with offences that might not be an offence in one jurisdiction, but is an offence in another.

Recommendation 38

- The relevant authority should take expeditious action in response to requests by foreign countries to identify, freeze, seize and confiscate property laundered or the proceeds from money laundering.
- There should also be arrangements for coordinating seizure and confiscation proceedings, which may include the sharing of confiscated assets.

This Recommendation simply takes cooperation from Recommendation 36 into the area of asset recovery.

Recommendation 39

- Countries should recognise money laundering as an extraditable offence.
- Each country should either extradite its own nationals, or where a country does not do so that country should, at the request of the country seeking extradition, submit the case without undue delay to its competent authorities for the purpose of prosecution.
- The countries concerned should cooperate with each other, in particular on procedural and evidentiary aspects, to ensure the efficiency of such prosecutions.
- Subject to their legal frameworks, countries may consider simplifying extradition by allowing direct transmission of extradition requests between appropriate ministries, extraditing persons based only on warrants of arrests or judgments, and/or introducing a simplified extradition of consenting persons who waive formal extradition proceedings.

Extradition law is another potential barrier to a successful international prosecution, and also an area where rules vary significantly between jurisdictions. This Recommendation makes it clear that the FATF does not want such legislation to become a barrier to prosecution.

Recommendation 40

- Countries should ensure that their competent authorities provide the widest possible range of international cooperation to their foreign counterparts.
- Countries should prompt exchange directly between counterparts, either spontaneously or upon request, of information relating to both money laundering and the underlying predicate offences.
- Exchanges should be permitted without unduly restrictive conditions. In particular:
  (a) Competent authorities should not refuse a request for assistance on the sole ground that the request is also considered to involve fiscal matters.
  (b) Countries should not invoke laws that require financial institutions to maintain secrecy or confidentiality as a ground for refusing to provide cooperation.
  (c) Competent authorities should be able to conduct inquiries, and where possible, investigations, on behalf of foreign counterparts.

- Countries are also encouraged to permit a prompt and constructive exchange of information with non counterparts. Cooperation with foreign authorities other than counterparts could occur directly or indirectly. When uncertain about the appropriate avenue to follow, competent authorities should first contact their foreign counterparts for assistance.
- Countries should establish controls and safeguards to ensure that information exchanged by competent authorities is used only in an authorised manner, consistent with their obligations concerning privacy and data protection.

This final Recommendation again relates to cooperation and tries to deal with the issue of tax evasion and represents another attack on offshore financial centres.

The 9 Special Recommendations

The FATF issued 9 Special Recommendations in October 2001 after the tragic events of September 11, 2001. They were introduced to help combat terrorist financing and aim to broadly extend the application of the 40 Recommendations to include terrorist financing and introduce new requirements relating to services such as alternative remittance, wire transfers and cash couriers as well as for non-profit making organisations, including charities.

Special Recommendation 1. Ratification and implementation of UN instruments

- Countries should immediately ratify and implement the 1999 United Nations International Convention for the Suppression of the Financing of Terrorism.
- Countries should also immediately implement the United Nations resolutions relating to the prevention and suppression of the financing of terrorist acts, particularly United Nations Security Council Resolution 1373.

This could have been achieved through a minor change to an existing recommendation.

Special Recommendation 2. Criminalising the financing of terrorism and associated money laundering

- Countries should criminalise the financing of terrorism, terrorist acts and terrorist organisations.

- Countries should ensure that such offences are designated as money laundering predicate offences.

This could also have been achieved through a minor change to the existing recommendations.

Special Recommendation 3. Freezing and confiscating terrorist assets

- Each country should implement measures to freeze without delay funds or other assets of terrorists and those who finance terrorism and terrorist organisations in accordance with the United Nations resolutions relating to the prevention and suppression of the financing of terrorist acts.
- Each country should also adopt and implement legislative measures, which would enable the competent authorities to seize and confiscate property that is connected to the financing of terrorism, terrorist acts or terrorist organisations.

This issue, that needs to be carefully addressed, is the definition of terrorist and terrorist organisation. Views can differ and policies and procedures need to carefully address such matters on an international basis. It is possible for a party to be considered legitimate in one group of countries while also being a terrorist organisation in others. Consequently such lists need to be kept up to date and regularly reviewed for completeness.

Special Recommendation 4. Reporting suspicious transactions related to terrorism

- Where any institution subject to anti-money laundering obligations, suspects or has reasonable grounds to suspect that funds are linked or related to, or are to be used for terrorism, terrorist acts or by terrorist organisations, they should be required to report promptly their suspicions to the competent authorities.

Again having included terrorist financing as a predicate offence, this effectively duplicates the original recommendation.

Special Recommendation 5. International cooperation

- Each country should afford another country the greatest possible measure of assistance in connection with criminal, civil enforcement, and administrative investigations, inquiries and proceedings relating to the financing of terrorism, terrorist acts and terrorist organisations.

- Countries should also take all possible measures to ensure that they do not provide safe havens for individuals charged with the financing of terrorism, terrorist acts or terrorist organisations, and should have procedures in place to extradite, where possible, such individuals.

It is the safe haven rules that are to some extent new. They seek to place an obligation on a jurisdiction not to have people or organisations that are charged with offences (not guilty of offences) even if such offences are not claimed to have been conducted in the "safe haven" country. This can run contrary to human rights legislation and therefore becomes a complex legal issue.

Special Recommendation 6. Alternative remittance

- Each country should take measures to ensure that persons or legal entities, including agents, that provide a service for the transmission of money or value, including transmission through an informal money or value transfer system or network, should be licensed or registered and subject to all the FATF Recommendations that apply to banks and non bank financial institutions.
- Each country should ensure that persons or legal entities that carry out this service illegally are subject to administrative, civil or criminal sanctions.

Again a minor clarification of the existing recommendations would have dealt with this issue. The concern was that unlicensed money transmission businesses may be used by inappropriate people.

Special Recommendation 7. Wire transfers

- Countries should take measures to require financial institutions, including money remitters, to include accurate and meaningful originator information (name, address and account number) on funds transfers and related messages that are sent, and the information should remain with the transfer or related message through the payment chain.
- Countries should take measures to ensure that financial institutions, including money remitters, conduct enhanced scrutiny of

and monitor for suspicious activity funds transfers which do not contain complete originator information (name, address and account number).

This does place additional requirements to counteract what was considered to be a systemic weakness in providing relevant information.

Special Recommendation 8. Nonprofit organisations

- Countries should review the adequacy of their laws and regulations that relate to entities that can be abused for the financing of terrorism.
- Nonprofit organisations are particularly vulnerable, and countries should ensure that they cannot be misused.

This is completely new, requiring reviews to be conducted into not-for-profit organisations which could potentially be used for money laundering. The level of work required varies considerably between jurisdictions.

Special Recommendation 9. Cash couriers

- Countries should have measures to detect the physical cross-border transportation of currency and bearer negotiable instruments, including a declaration system or other disclosure obligation.
- Countries should ensure that their competent authorities have the legal authority to stop or restrain currency or bearer negotiable instruments that are suspected to be related to terrorist financing or money laundering, or that are falsely declared or disclosed.
- Countries should ensure that competent authorities are available to deal with persons who make false declaration(s) or disclosure(s).
- In cases where the currency or bearer negotiable instruments are related to terrorist financing or money laundering, countries should adopt effective, proportionate and dissuasive sanctions as well as measures which would enable the confiscation of such currency or instruments.

Obviously monies moving across borders could be inappropriate, therefore FATF have introduced these requirements, which are broader than the requirements in the original Recommendations.

As you can see in composite the 40 Recommendations and the Special Recommendations do create a general environment of expectation within which individual jurisdictions can draft their legal structure and provide advice and guidance to relevant institutions. What this actually means in practice is further explained throughout this book.

Chapter 3

EUROPE – THE THIRD MONEY LAUNDERING DIRECTIVE

BACKGROUND TO THE DIRECTIVE

The various European Union (EU) money laundering directives are the way in which the EU incorporates FATF's international standards in order to provide consolidated money laundering legislation, while at the same time highlighting specific additional concerns which are of interest to EU law makers. As with all EU directives, the onus is on national governments to transform these requirements into local law.

The First Money Laundering Directive (1991) focused on combating the laundering of drug proceeds through the financial sector. Specific obligations were placed on firms in the financial sector and the Directive introduced requirements relating to the obligation to maintain systems for customer identification, staff training, record keeping, and the reporting of suspicious transactions.

The Second Money Laundering Directive (2001) amended the First Money Laundering Directive by introducing changes in two main areas. Firstly, it expanded the scope of predicate offences for which suspicious transaction reporting was mandatory from drug trafficking to all serious offences. Secondly, it also extended the scope of the Directive to include a number of nonfinancial activities and professions including lawyers, notaries, accountants, estate agents, art dealers, jewellers, auctioneers and casinos.

The final text of the Third EC Directive was published in the official journal of the European Union on 25 November 2005. Member States had until 15 December 2007 to implement the Directive. Many countries have already implemented the Directive whilst some are yet to fully implement the Directive.[1]

AIMS OF THE DIRECTIVE

The Third Directive notes that money laundering by its very nature is an international problem and thus must be addressed on an inter-

---

[1]The text of the Directive may be found on the following web link: Implementation: http://eur-lex.europa.eu/LexUriServ/site/en/oj/2006/l_214/l_21420060804en00290034.pdf. Original directive: http://eur-lex.europa.eu/LexUriServ/LexUriServ.do?uri=OJ:L:2005:309:0015:0036:EN:PDF. For further information on the UK implementation, look to the following reference: http://www.fsa.gov.uk/pages/About/What/International/pdf/TMLD.pdf.

national level. It recognises that measures adopted on a national level can never fully counter money laundering activity. Consequently international coordination and cooperation is needed so that consistent action taken at an international level can effectively combat money laundering and terrorist financing. The European Community has taken particular account of the FATF Recommendations to provide a base in order to achieve their objectives.

The Third Directive provides a common basis for implementing the revised FATF Recommendations which were introduced in June 2003. The new Recommendations now take into account the new risks and practices which have developed since the previous Directive (the Second Directive). It is also the aim of the UK's regulatory body, the Financial Services Authority, and other international regulatory bodies to implement a risk-based approach to combating money laundering. The Third Directive also seeks to ensure that these new requirements are feasible, proportionate and justified by cost–benefit analysis.

THE UK IMPLEMENTATION OF THE DIRECTIVE

The Third Directive on Money Laundering was implemented into UK law on 15 December 2007 by the Money Laundering Regulations 2007. The Joint Money Laundering Steering Group (JMLSG) produced guidance to reflect the changes to the UK's legal framework as a result of the implementation of the Directive, as these were now legally binding. In many cases financial firms were already adopting the measures the Money Laundering Regulations 2007 had made mandatory.

KEY PROVISIONS OF THE DIRECTIVE

The new Directive recommended a number of changes. Some of the changes were new, whilst others developed and amended previous provisions. This section will look at key provisions which brought about substantial change and also the key provisions the Third Directive recommends that Member States implement. These key provisions will thus either be incorporated into domestic legislation of EU Member States directly as seen in most of the relevant EU country legislation, or used as guidance.

For countries outside of the EU the Third Directive can, to some extent, be considered as international best practice and therefore it remains of interest. It also provides information relevant for financial institutions in overseas jurisdictions that are dealing with institutions and customers based within the EU.

OVERVIEW OF THE DIRECTIVE

The Third Directive is actually Directive 2005/60/EC of the European Parliament and of the Council of 26 October 2005 ("the Directive") on the prevention and use of the financial system for the purpose of money laundering and terrorist financing. In this section we provide some brief details of the Directive, but for full information you will still need to refer to the Directive itself.

Scope of the Directive

Paragraph 8 of the guidance in the Directive extends the purpose of scope of the Directive to also combat the financing of terrorism. As such it is picking up the 9 Special Recommendations that FATF issued in the aftermath of September 11. As with any EU directive there is a clear political element and in this case the Directive states that the misuse of the financial system to channel criminal or even clean money to terrorist purposes represents a clear risk to the integrity, proper functioning, reputation and stability of the financial system. Accordingly the preventative measures in the Directive should cover not only the manipulation of money derived from crime but also the collection of money for terrorist purposes.

The Directive defines "terrorist financing" as the provision or collection of funds, by any means, directly or indirectly, with the intention that they should be used or in the knowledge that they are to be used, in full or in part, in order to carry out any of the predicate or criminal offences. Of course again we have the problem that a terrorist in one country might be considered a freedom fighter in another – and of course such organisations do change over time. Accordingly it will always be worth checking whether a particular body is considered as a terrorist organisation at a particular point in time.

1. What is considered to be money laundering

The Directive has the requirement that Member States must essentially ensure that money laundering and terrorist financing are prohibited to the maximum extent feasible. Of course this sounds fine in principle but in practice would be difficult to comply with. The maximum extent feasible might be so onerous as to impact legitimate activity – indeed it is the legitimate customer that is often put at a disadvantage by such regulation.

The Directive states that the following, when committed intentionally, shall be regarded as "money laundering":

(a) The conversion or transfer of property, knowing that such property is derived from criminal activity or from an act of participation in such activity, for the purpose of concealing or disguising the illicit origin of the property or of assisting any person who is involved in the commission of such activity to evade the legal consequences of his action. Consequently it is clear that failing to provide information or assisting a family member to enable them to escape prosecution would be considered as money laundering. Likewise assisting a firm to provide financial statements that are inaccurate might also be caught by such rules.

(b) The concealment or disguising of the true nature, source, location, disposition, movement, rights with respect to, or ownership of property, knowing that such property is derived from criminal activity or an act of participation in such activity. While this requirement is quite broad there is in this case still the requirement for knowledge although in some jurisdictions there is the assumption that there should have been knowledge which impacts the "ignorance" defence.

(c) The acquisition, possession or use of property, knowing at the time of receipt that such property was derived from criminal activity or an act of participation in such activity. Consequently if you did not know then you would not be guilty of an offence. For example if someone sells you a stolen car without you being suspicious and you then sell it on to a third party you would not be guilty of money laundering if you did not know at the time that the car had been stolen. This can be a useful "get out of jail" card since it would require the enforcement agencies to prove knowledge beyond reasonable doubt to get a prosecution.

(d) Participation in, association to commit, attempts to commit and aiding, abetting, facilitating and counselling the commission of any of the actions mentioned in the foregoing points. This means that you do not actually need to be successful – even if you tried to commit the crime you would clearly be guilty.

Terrorist Financing means the provision or collection of funds, by any means, directly or indirectly, with the intention that they should be used or in the knowledge that they are to be used, in full or in part, in order to carry out any of the offences within the meanings of Article 1-4 of Council Framework Decision 2002/474/JHA of 13 June 2002 on combating terrorism. This has the effect of drawing the rules extremely broadly and you might notice that it includes indirect means. For example if you allowed your name to be used to encourage a person to provide funds to a terrorist organisation then you would clearly still be guilty of an offence even though you might not know the person approached.

The Directive states that knowledge, intent or purpose, for the purposes of the above definitions, may be inferred from objective factual circumstances. This puts the onus onto the local agencies and financial institutions to undertake such work as they consider appropriate to build up a case based on the balance of probability. It does say objective factual information and therefore rumour and supposition would not be sufficient.

The Directive does include some useful definitions for each of the following:

- credit institutions
- financial institutions
- property
- criminal activity
- serious crime
- beneficial owners, including corporate entities
- trust and company service providers
- politically exposed persons
- business relationship
- shell bank.

However there is no requirement for anyone to actually use these definitions and in practice many jurisdictions use their own definitions which are consistent with local rules and regulations.

2. Application

The Directive has widened the application of the Second Directive to include all of the following:

1. credit institutions
2. financial institutions
3. legal and natural persons exercising professional activities including:
   (a) auditors, external accountants and tax advisors
   (b) notaries and other independent legal professionals when they participate in acting on behalf of and for their client in any financial or real estate transaction, or by assisting in the planning and execution of transactions for their clients concerning:
      (i) buying and selling of real estate, property or business entities
      (ii) managing of client money, securities or other assets
      (iii) opening or management of bank, savings or securities accounts
      (iv) organisation of contributions necessary for the creating, operation or management of trusts companies or similar structures
   (c) trust or company service providers
   (d) real estate agents
   (e) other natural or legal persons trading in goods where payments are made in cash in the amount of EUR 15 000 or more, whether in a single or linked transaction
   (f) casinos.

This is a major broadening of the types of business that are now caught by the rules and in particular catches quite a few consultancy and accounting firms. The managing client money rules will in many cases broaden the net to include fund management firms that might have been left out in some jurisdictions. The objectives are clear in that the Directive is seeking to ensure that anyone moving significant sums is now to be identified and reviewed. Whether such bodies have actually been involved with money laundering identification is not the issue to concern you – they are now part of the regime and will need to comply. The only question is, who is the relevant authority in such cases?

There is even a wider "catch-all" provision. Member States can extend the provisions of the Directive in whole to professions and to any category of undertaking which engages in activities likely to be used for money laundering or terrorist financing purposes.

3. Customer due diligence

When should a firm carry out due diligence?

The general requirement to conduct due diligence applies in the following cases:

(a) when establishing a business relationship;
(b) when carrying out occasional transactions amounting to EUR 15 000 or more, whether the transaction is carried out in a single operation or several operations which appear to be linked;
(c) when there is suspicion of money laundering or terrorist financing regardless of any derogation, exemption or threshold;
(d) when there are doubts about the adequacy of previously obtained customer identification.

We shall consider this in more detail later. Notice that the primary responsibility is at the start of the relationship. Of course money launderers and terrorist financers will know this and accordingly will attempt to appear as legitimate at the start of the relationship, undertaking inappropriate activity at a later stage. As we shall see there are also ongoing monitoring requirements.

What due diligence measures are required?

There is a list of required due diligence procedures in the Directive which do tend to form the basis for requirements in European States. These are as follows:

(a) Identifying the customer and verifying the customer's identification on the basis of documents, data or information obtained from a reliable and independent source. Notice the requirement here is for independent sources so you should not just accept documents provided to you by the customer – if they are undertaking criminal activity they are likely to have perfect documents which are actually themselves forged. Some form of independent confirmation should, where possible, be obtained.

(b) Identifying, where applicable, the beneficial owner of the account and using risk-based measures to verify identity so that the institution is satisfied that it knows who the beneficial owner is, including trusts and similar legal arrangements. This will include taking risk-based measures to understand the ownership and control structure of the customer. The importance of beneficial ownership is that the person appearing as the owner may actually just be acting on behalf of the actual owner. As such they may be partners in law firms or similar service providers. The information required is who is really behind the transactions since they are more likely to be the criminal elements.

This should take place before the establishment of a business relationship or the carrying out of any transaction. To fulfil this requirement a firm or person can decide whether they make use of public records of beneficial owners, or whether they ask their clients for relevant data or information, or how else they obtain sufficient details to provide themselves with adequate due diligence information. In other words they can almost do whatever they like.

(c) Obtaining information on the purpose and intended nature of the business relationship. This is required to enable the firm to subsequently identify transactions which are inconsistent with the purpose of the relationship to enable suspicious transactions to be identified.

(d) Conducting ongoing monitoring of the business relationship including scrutiny of transactions undertaken to ensure that they are consistent with the institution's or person's knowledge of the customer, the business and risk profile. This review should include obtaining information, where necessary, of the source of funds and ensuring that documents, data or information held are kept up-to-date. There is actually no requirement to obtain independent evidence of the source of funds, just to record the source of funds. For example if the customer says they sold a car and received cash, there is no requirement to see that they actually ever had a car and whether it could have been worth the amount of funds received. All the firm would need to do is record that they received cash from the sale of a car.

The issue of legal confidentiality

Where notaries, independent legal professionals, auditors, external accountants and tax advisors are in the course of ascertaining the legal position for their client or defending or representing their client in judicial proceedings or advice on instituting or avoiding proceedings they do not need to comply with these requirements. This is to make sure that the legal process is not prejudiced and also to enable the "expert" to discuss matters with their client appropriately. If they had to make a report every time their client said something that might be considered as illegal, then the whole process under which the legal profession operates could have been undermined.

Enhanced due diligence

Enhanced due diligence is required in all cases where the situation represents a higher money laundering or terrorist financing risk. Such procedures will apply particularly for non face-to-face business, politically exposed persons and international correspondent banking relationships. The Directive does provide some basic guidance, but we expand on this further later in this book.

The problems of non face-to-face customers

Where the customer has not been physically present for identification purposes, firms should apply one or more of the following measures:

1. Ensure that the customer's identity is established beyond reasonable doubt by obtaining additional documents, data or information.
2. Undertake supplementary measures to verify or certify the documents supplied.
3. Ensure that the first payment is carried out through an account opened in the customer's name with a credit institution.

Whilst the Directive states "one or more", in most cases we are finding that the expectation is that all three measures will be adopted unless there is a good reason why one or other is unsuitable in the circumstances. Even this is not ideal – identification documents that show a picture cannot be compared to the actual customer themselves since they are never met.

The problems of international correspondent banking

In respect of cross-frontier correspondent banking relationships with respondent institutions from third countries, the requirements are for credit institutions to:

1. Gather sufficient information about a respondent institution to understand fully the nature of the respondent's business and to

determine from publically available information the reputation of the institution and the quality of supervision applied locally. This information is generally available in the market and regulatory structures are even ranked by independent bodies to provide additional third party analysis.

2. Assess the respondent institution's anti-money laundering and anti-terrorist financing controls. This is rather harder to obtain other than directly from the firm itself. Even then it will not be clear which of the policies and procedures presented are actually being complied with.

3. Obtain approval from senior management before establishing new correspondent banking relationships. This will at least ensure that someone within the business has considered whether the relationship really is appropriate for the brand.

4. Document the respective responsibilities of each institution with regard to money laundering deterrence. As a general rule firms now rarely rely directly on work being conducted by a third party and often repeat such work for themselves.

5. With respect to payable-through accounts, be satisfied that the respondent credit institution has verified the identity of and performed ongoing due diligence on the customers having direct access to accounts of the correspondent and that it is able to provide relevant customer due diligence data to the correspondent institution upon request. This is to deal with cases where the customer is only passing through the correspondent relationship – clearly an area of potential money laundering. Whether it is actually even legal to provide the due diligence materials maintained will depend on the individual country rules and this could inhibit the effectiveness of this rule.

Of course trying to apply these rules within Europe where all countries in principle have implemented the same rules is rather different from applying them in non European markets where different standards apply.

The problems with politically exposed persons

A "politically exposed person" (PEP), is defined as someone who is or has been entrusted with prominent public functions and their immediate family members, together with persons known to be their close associates.

In respect of transactions or business relationships with politically exposed persons residing in another Member State or in a third country, the requirement is for a firm to:

1. have appropriate risk-based procedures to determine whether the customer is a politically exposed person;
2. have senior management approval for establishing business relationships with such customers;
3. take adequate measures to establish the source of wealth and source of funds that are involved in a business relationship or transaction;
4. conduct enhanced ongoing monitoring of the business relationship.

As you will see, the definition is people that have been or are in office, therefore someone that has run for office, but not been elected, is not a PEP. Whilst this is what is stated in the Directive and is normally what has been transcribed into national law, it may well not be sufficient to provide the level of protection that a firm requires. Accordingly many firms are adopting a wider definition that provides for additional investigation of a broader group of customers. The level of confirmation of wealth is clearly an issue and in such cases just asking the customer cannot be sufficient. You know what the concerns are – that the politically exposed person may have taken advantage of their position to increase their personal wealth. Additional enquiries independent of the customer will be required to meet these demands.

The problems of anonymous accounts

There is particular concern over products or transactions that might favour anonymity. Effectively the requirements here are trying to prevent firms using numbered accounts or other secrecy approaches which may inhibit the identification of the actual or beneficial owner of an account. Basically any firm should know the identity of the beneficial owners of all accounts.

The problems of casinos

Everything we have looked at so far in the Directive is related to banks and other types of financial institution. This section is rather different. There is a requirement that all casino customers should be identified and their identity verified if they purchase or exchange gambling chips with a value of EUR 2000 or more. Casinos subject to state intervention shall be deemed in any event to have satisfied the customer due diligence requirements if they register, identify and verify the identity of their customers immediately on, or before, entry regardless of the amount of gambling chips purchased.

The requirement is easy to put into place, but the level of actual monitoring will be dependent upon the agencies that verify compliance by the casino. Of course casinos are perfect for money laundering. You take cash in to the casino – there is no reason to say where the funds are from. You provide some identification documentation – there is no need to provide secondary identification. You purchase your chips and then go for a meal. Then you cash in your chips and receive laundered money. Perhaps this is a true case of having your chips and eating them! At least this is a starting point for effective regulation of the casino industry, although such regulation does vary considerably between jurisdictions.

What is simplified due diligence?

Simplified due diligence was introduced as an exemption to full due diligence where the customer is a credit or financial institution covered by the Directive or a credit or financial institution situated in a third country which imposes equivalent requirements and is appropriately supervised.

No requirement for due diligence at all!!

The Directive does not require customer due diligence to be conducted (at Member State discretion) in respect of:

1. Listed companies whose securities are admitted to trading on a regulated market which are subject to disclosure requirements consistent with Community legislation. This is because they will have been verified by the listing authority. Of course the firm will still need to confirm that the company is that listed firm – and not a firm trying to steal their identity.

2. Beneficial owners of pooled accounts held by notaries and other independent legal professionals, provided that they are subject to requirements to combat money laundering or terrorist financing consistent with international standards, and are supervised for compliance. There is also a requirement that they will provide information on the identity of the beneficial owner, on request to the institution that acts as the depository institution for the pooled

accounts. Again this exception is because the notary is under the identification obligation and has been reviewed in this regard by their regulator.

3. Domestic public authorities because they clearly could never be guilty of money laundering. I would not expect any firm not to wish to identify the public authority if only to ensure that there are no political issues which they need to be aware of. The politically exposed person rules will still probably require due diligence to be conducted.

4. Customers representing a low risk of money laundering or terrorist financing purely because the regulators would wish the financial institution to concentrate on areas which are more likely to represent a significant risk. Such an example might include payments taken directly from a salary by an employer. The financial institution would know exactly where the funds were from and who they were held by – clearly representing a very low risk of money laundering.

5. Life insurance policies where the annual premium is no more than EUR 1000 or the single premium is no more than EUR 2500. While this could be used for money laundering the view is taken that the level of funds laundered would render this cumbersome and expensive for the launderer to manage and accordingly the risk posed to the system is low.

6. Insurance policies of pension schemes if there is no surrender clause and the policy cannot be used as collateral since it would be difficult to launder through such instruments. The absence of a surrender clause is key in coming to such a decision.

7. A pension, superannuation or similar scheme that provides retirement benefits to employees, where contributions are made by way of deduction from wages and the scheme rules do not permit the assignment of a member's interest under the scheme.

This is really all about applying the risk-based approach to supervision and investigation. What the Directive is actually saying is that these types of product or service are not really suitable for money laundering or terrorist financing and therefore it would be onerous to impose the same level of regulation on them. Notice for example the references to surrender clauses or value. Surrender clauses can be used by money launderers, but in the absence of such a clause it is difficult to see how the product could be suitable for the criminal fraternity.

4. Reporting obligations

The main obligation here is to create a Financial Intelligence Unit (FIU). Reporting should concentrate on transactions which are particularly likely, by their nature, to be related to money laundering or terrorist financing, together with particularly complex or unusually large transactions and any unusual patterns of transactions which have no apparent economic or visible purpose.

Such suspicious transactions must be reported to the relevant Financial Intelligence Unit. The unit will be responsible for receiving, requesting, analysing and disseminating to the competent authorities, and for disclosure of information which concerns potential money laundering, potential terrorist financing or is otherwise required. The FIU must have access to the financial administrative and law enforcement information that it requires to properly fulfil its tasks.

There is a safe harbour here for the reporting employee at the financial institution. The disclosure of information by an employee or director of an institution does not constitute a breach of any restriction on the disclosure of information imposed by contract or by any legislative, regulatory or administrative provision, and shall not involve the institution or person or its directors or employees in liability of any kind. This protects the whistleblower and enables (indeed perhaps even encourages) reporting of relevant information.

5. Tipping off

There is an important prohibition from disclosing to customers or third persons (other than regulators) the fact that information has been transmitted to the relevant FIU or that a money laundering or terrorist financing investigation is being or may be carried out.

This effectively enshrines the principle of tipping off, which therefore becomes an offence. Clearly tipping off, as we shall discuss later, is a significant risk for any investigator and limits both the questions that may be asked and also the way in which they are posed.

6. Record keeping

In terms of record keeping, the requirements are as follows:

(a) Customer due diligence – a copy of, or the references requested of, the evidence required for a period of at least five years after the business relationship with their customer has ended.
(b) Business relationships and transactions – the supporting evidence and records, consisting of the original documents or copies admissible in court proceedings under the applicable national legislation for a period of at least five years following the carrying out of the transactions or the end of the business relationship.

7. Internal procedures, training and feedback (Articles 34–35)

Institutions and persons covered by the Directive must establish adequate and appropriate policies and procedures for the following:

(a) customer due diligence
(b) reporting
(c) record keeping
(d) internal control
(e) risk assessment
(f) risk management
(g) compliance management
(h) communication in order to prevent operations related to money laundering or terrorist financing.

They must also communicate relevant policies and procedures to branches and majority owned subsidiaries in third countries. There is also a requirement that relevant training must be provided for relevant employees. This may involve participation in special ongoing training programmes to help them recognise which operations may be related to money laundering and terrorist financing and instruct them how to proceed with such cases.

The requirements regarding training and understanding money laundering and terrorist financing are clearly crucial. By emphasising the importance of understanding how the criminal operates the Directive is seeking to improve both the quality of skills within the deterrence industry and also perhaps the introduction of more thoughtful detection of inappropriate activity.

8. Supervision

Broadening the nature of firms caught by the Regulations, there is a requirement for currency exchange offices, money transmission or remittance offices and trust and company service providers and casinos to be licensed or registered and licensed to operate their business legally.

The key issues here relate to the extension of the regime to additional types of organisation. Trust and company services areas are the major field where approaches differ between countries. Clearly an organisation has to be designated to monitor adherence to these obligations and then have the skills and staff necessary to undertake such work.

If you are a trust or company service company then you will need to see if you fall within the structure of your local rules and regulations and, if so, identify the body with which you are required to register. With such registration there is likely to be a series of additional responsibilities and requirements with which you will have to comply. These will then need to be expressly transferred into the rules and regulations of your firm and notified as appropriate to your relevant employees and, where relevant, clients.

9. Penalties

The Directive provides for the right to impose penalties that are effective, proportionate and dissuasive.

10. Risk-based approach

As set out earlier, the Directive recognises the concept of a risk-based/risk-sensitive approach to anti-money laundering. Accordingly the implementation of a risk-based approach is encouraged throughout various provisions of the Directive, particularly, as we have seen, in the due diligence requirements. This is to ensure that institutions direct their attention and resources to those areas which are most likely to identify cases of inappropriate activity.

The principle is that actual customer due diligence requirements may be determined on a risk-sensitive basis depending on the type of customer, business relationship, product or transaction. However there is the requirement of being able to demonstrate that the extent of the measures is appropriate in view of the risks of money laundering and terrorist financing.

The effect of the clarifying requirements is to make the risk-based approach more carefully applied in practice. Institutions will be required to document their approaches in clear guidance notes and policies and procedures within their organisation. Such procedures will then need to be rigorously followed in practice to justify the appropriateness requirement.

Always recognise that the Directive only provides an outline and will always need to be supplemented by additional local guidance, together with being transcribed into local law. As such, while it provides the framework, it cannot provide the details due to the differences inherent in local rules, regulations and structures. In the detailed chapters of this book we look at some of the specific areas where additional guidance is required and set out the key issues that will need to be considered.

Chapter 4

THE UK REGULATORY FRAMEWORK

BACKGROUND

In the UK financial services regulation has travelled through a series of routes to arrive at the current position, which itself is certain to change. Initially regulation in the UK for banking was the clear responsibility of the Bank of England, with their powers being enshrined in a series of banking laws and their guidance published in various regulations.

This changed with the development of broader financial services regulation as a result of the implementation of the Financial Services Act 1986. This did not really change the responsibilities of the Bank of England which remained a full central bank with responsibility for the regulation of banks, but introduced the Securities and Investments Board. The Board did very little direct regulation, but did ensure that a series of industry-based regulators achieved the standards of regulation that they required. Effectively this enshrined the principle of self regulation which became a driver for UK financial services regulation for a decade. The Securities and Investments Board was essentially replaced by the Financial Services Authority (FSA), which also took over the responsibilities for the majority of the self-regulatory bodies that previously existed (for example the Personal Investment Authority and the Investment Managers Regulatory Organisation).[1]

THE FINANCIAL SERVICES AND MARKETS ACT 2000

The Financial Services and Markets Act (FSMA) sets out the current structure of financial service regulation in the UK. The Act's main objectives are:

- to create a single statutory regulator – the Financial Services Authority (FSA);
- to set out the statutory powers for the FSA;
- to define the statutory objectives of the FSA.

---

[1]At the time of writing consideration is being given to changing the structure of regulatory bodies in the United Kingdom. This is likely to change the body responsible for certain elements of the UK regime, but is unlikely to make any substantial changes to the nature of the regulatory structure for money laundering deterrence and terrorist financing.

FSMA 2000 imposes four key statutory objectives on the FSA:

1. Maintaining confidence in the UK financial system.
2. Promoting public understanding of the financial system, which will include awareness of the benefits and risks associated with different kinds of investments and providing appropriate information and advice.
3. Securing the appropriate level of protection for consumers considering:
   (a) differing levels of risk that come with different kinds of investment;
   (b) differing levels of consumer experience and expertise;
   (c) the need for accurate advice and information.
4. Reducing financial crime.

It is unusual for a main financial service regulator to have financial crime reduction as a primary purpose and, when combined with the second "treating customers fairly" objective, does result in the FSA's rulebook being different in nature to many international regulatory rule books, both in terms of its structure and its contents.

The Bank of England does retain responsibility for the money supply, but it does not at this time have any responsibility in respect of the regulation of banks. This is a situation which is likely to change.

FIT AND PROPER PERSON RULES

The FSMA introduces the regulatory framework through the General Prohibition, which states that "no person may carry out a regulated activity in the UK unless they are an authorised or an exempt person". Therefore, firms and individuals who work for firms must be approved by the FSA. In order to be approved by the FSA individuals responsible must be "fit and proper", which means that they are considered appropriate people to be involved with such a significant role.

Individuals will be considered to be "fit and proper" by the FSA in relation to the following:

- honesty, integrity and reputation;
- competence and capacity;
- financial soundness.

Within the rule book of the Financial Services Authority the regulations promulgated by the Joint Money Laundering Steering Group (Chapter 7) are adopted as best practice. No separate detailed guidance regarding money laundering deterrence and terrorist financing appears within the FSA Handbook, although as we shall see there is some outline guidance available.

FSA REGULATION AND MONEY LAUNDERING DETERRENCE

As we have seen, the Financial Services and Markets Act (FSMA) gives the FSA a statutory objective to reduce crime. In considering these objectives the FSA is required to have regard to firms:

- being aware of the risk of their business being used in connection with the commission of financial crime;
- taking appropriate measures to prevent financial crime, facilitate its detection and monitor its incidence;
- devoting adequate resources to that prevention, detection and monitoring.

The FSA's outline requirements relating to money laundering were initially contained in a separate Money Laundering sourcebook. Many of the requirements contained in the sourcebook have now been consolidated by the FSA into the FSA's Senior Management Arrangements, Systems and Controls (SYSC) rules. This approach has enabled firms to have more discretion when choosing to adopt anti-money laundering practices. Guidelines relating to money laundering contained in SYSC include the following:

- A firm must take care to establish and maintain effective systems and controls for countering the risk that it might be used for financial crime.
- A firm must ensure that these systems and controls enable it to identify, assess, monitor and manage money laundering risk (and are comprehensive and proportionate to the firm's activities). It must carry out regular assessments of the adequacy of these systems and controls.
- A firm may also be under separate obligations to comply with the relevant legal requirements, including the Terrorism Act, the Proceeds of Crime Act 2002 and the Money Laundering Regulations.
- In assessing whether a firm has been in breach of the SYSC requirements on money laundering, the FSA will have regard to

whether the firm has followed the Joint Money Laundering Steering Group (JMLSG) Guidance (see Chapter 5).

- The firm should ensure that its systems and controls include:
  - appropriate training for its employees in relation to money laundering;
  - appropriate provision for information to the board and senior management including an annual report by the firm's MLRO on the operation and effectiveness of systems and controls;
  - the responsibility within the firm for establishing and maintaining effective anti-money laundering systems and controls must be allocated to a director or senior manager who may be the MLRO.

The regulatory structure under which UK money laundering deterrence and terrorist financing legislation operates is considered in the following sections.

THE PROCEEDS OF CRIME ACT 2002

The Proceeds of Crime Act 2002 (POCA) consolidates and extends the existing UK legislation regarding money laundering. The legislation covers all crimes and any dealing in criminal property, with no exceptions and unusually no de minimis. The effect of this is that any theft or other criminal offence regardless of value is in principle subject to these rules. The POCA has three main objectives:

1. It establishes the Assets Recovery Agency to conduct an investigation to discover whether a person holds criminal assets and to recover the assets in question.
2. It creates five investigative powers for the law enforcement agencies:
   - a production order
   - a search and seizure order
   - a disclosure order
   - a customer information order
   - an account monitoring order.
3. It establishes the following criminal offences:
   - To acquire, use, possess, conceal, disguise, convert, transfer or remove criminal property from the jurisdiction, or to enter into or become involved in an arrangement to facilitate the acquisition, retention, use or control of criminal property by another person.

- For persons working in the regulated sector of failing to make a report where they have knowledge or suspicion of money laundering or reasonable grounds for having knowledge or suspicion that another person is laundering the proceeds of any criminal conduct, as soon as is reasonably practical after the information came to their attention in the course of their regulated business activities.
- For anyone to take any action likely to prejudice an investigation by informing (tipping off) the person who is the subject of a suspicious report, that a report has been made to a nominated officer or to The Serious Organised Crime Agency (SOCA), or that the police or customs authorities are carrying out or intend to carry out a money laundering investigation.
- Of destroying or disposing of documents which are relevant to an investigation.
- Of failing to comply with a requirement imposed on it under a customer information order, or in knowingly or recklessly making a statement in purported compliance with a customer information order that is false or misleading in a material particular.

4. POCA also sets out the maximum penalties as follows:
   - For the offence of money laundering of 14 years' imprisonment and/or an unlimited fine. However an offence is not committed if the offence was reported to SOCA as soon as was reasonably practical.
   - For failing to make a report of suspected money laundering or for tipping off of five years' imprisonment and/or an unlimited fine.
   - For destroying or disposing of relevant documents of five years' imprisonment and/or an unlimited fine.

The Proceeds of Crime Act is just one of the many laws which impacts on money laundering and terrorist financing. It needs to be considered in terms of its impact on other relevant regulation.

THE TERRORISM ACT 2000 AND THE ANTI-TERRORISM CRIME AND SECURITY ACT 2001

The Terrorism Act 2000 establishes a series of offences related to the involvement of persons or organisations in arrangements for facilitating, raising or using funds for terrorist purposes.

1. The Terrorism Act sets out the following criminal offences:
   - For any person not to report the existence of terrorist property where there are reasonable grounds for knowing or suspecting the existence of terrorist property.
   - For anyone to take any action likely to prejudice an investigation by informing (i.e. tipping off) the person who is the subject of a suspicion report, or anybody else that a disclosure has been made to a nominated officer or to the SOCA, or that the police or customs authorities are carrying out or intending to carry out a terrorist financing investigation.

   The parallels to the POCA are clearly to be seen with the general wording being both consistent and similar.
2. The Terrorism Act then sets out the following penalties:
   - The maximum penalty for failure to report under the circumstances set out above is five years' imprisonment and/or an unlimited fine.
   - The maximum penalty for the offence of actual money laundering is 14 years' imprisonment and/or a unlimited fine.

   Again these are consistent with the approach adopted by the POCA.

The Anti-terrorism Crime and Security Act 2001 gives the authorities power to seize terrorist cash, to freeze terrorist assets and to direct firms in the regulated sector to provide the authorities with specified information on customers and their (terrorism-related) activities. As such it implements those of the 9 Special Recommendations of the Financial Actions Task Force (FATF) not already implemented into UK legislation.

THE MONEY LAUNDERING REGULATIONS 2007

The Money Laundering Regulations 2007 specify arrangements which must be in place within firms within the scope of the Regulations, in order to prevent operations relating to money laundering or terrorist financing.

The scope of the Regulations

In terms of their scope, the Money Laundering Regulations apply, inter alia, to:

- the regulated activities of all financial sector firms which include:
  - banks, building societies and other credit institutions;
  - individuals and firms engaged in regulated investment activities under the Financial Services and Markets Act 2000 (FSMA);
  - issuers of electronic money;
  - insurance companies undertaking long-term life business, including the life business of Lloyds of London;
- bureaux de change, cheque encashment centres and money transmission services;
- trust and company service providers;
- casinos;
- dealers in high-value goods (including auctioneers) who accept payment in cash of EUR 15 000 or more, whether this is a single or linked transaction;
- lawyers and accountants when undertaking relevant business.

The key requirements

Persons who are subject to the Money Laundering Regulations are required to establish adequate and appropriate policies and procedures in order to prevent operations relating to money laundering or terrorist financing covering:

- customer due diligence
- reporting
- record-keeping
- internal control
- risk assessment and management
- compliance management
- communications.

The FSA institutes proceedings for offences committed under the Regulations against both regulated and nonregulated firms. A breach of the Money Laundering Regulations is not dependant on whether money laundering has actually taken place. Firms can be sanctioned for not having adequate anti-money laundering and counter-terrorist funding systems. Failure to comply with any of the Money Laundering Regulations constitutes a punishable offence by a maximum of two years' imprisonment, a fine or both.

As you can see these broadly address the issues set out in the EU Third Directive as discussed in Chapter 3.

Chapter 5

HOW RULES ARE APPLIED IN THE UK – THE JOINT MONEY LAUNDERING STEERING GROUP

In the UK the guidance with regard to money laundering deterrence and terrorist financing is produced by the Joint Money Laundering Steering Group (JMLSG), which is made up of the leading UK Trade Associations in the Financial Services Industry, including the British Bankers' Association. Its existence actually predates the creation of the UK's unitary regulator, the Financial Services Authority. The aim of the JMLSG is to encourage good practice in countering money laundering and to give practical assistance in interpreting the statutory UK Money Laundering Regulations. This is primarily achieved by the publication of industry guidance which offers advice on suitable ways to comply with laws and regulations on financial crime. It also highlights areas of concern and suggests processes and procedures that should be considered.

It is important to note that the UK has statutory provisions and therefore any breach of the Regulations represents a criminal rather than a civil matter.

The rules themselves have been through many changes over the years and have both increased and decreased in their depth and scope. Initially drafted by experts in each individual field of financial services (the so-called coloured books), the rules have now been consolidated and reflect the UK's interpretation of relevant EU legislation as implemented into UK law incorporating FATF Guidance.

Guidance is only issued by the JMLSG after it has been approved by HM Treasury and as such UK courts must take the Guidance into account in the event of any legal proceedings. Adherence to the Guidance is also regarded by the Financial Services Authority (FSA) as demonstrating compliance with their relevant systems and controls rules. As such the FSA has effectively taken the totality of the JMLSG Guidance and incorporated it into their own rule book.

MEMBERSHIP

The JMLSG is made up of the leading UK Trade Associations in the financial services industry. As of November 2009, these consisted of the following organisations:

Asset Based Finance Association (ABSA)
Association of British Credit Unions Ltd (ABCUL)
Association of British Insurers (ABI)
Association of Foreign Banks (AFB)
Association of Friendly Societies (AFS)

Association of Independent Financial Advisers (AIFA)
Association of Private Client Investment Managers and Stockbrokers (APCIMS)
British Bankers' Association (BBA)
British Venture Capital Association (BVCA)
Building Societies Association (BSA)
Council of Mortgage Lenders (CML)
Electronic Money Association (EMA)
Finance & Leasing Association (FLA)
Futures and Options Association (FOA)
Investment Management Association (IMA)
London Investment Banking Association (LIBA)
Tax Incentivised Savings Association (TISA)
Wholesale Market Brokers' Association (WMBA).

The breadth of the organisations represented provides a warning as to the scope of money laundering regulation in the UK. In addition other organisations, whilst not being direct members, have attendance rights including bodies such as the Institute of Chartered Accountants in England and Wales, the equivalent bodies in Scotland and in Ireland and both the Institute and Faculties of Actuaries. The JMLSG has been producing Money Laundering Guidance for the financial sector since 1990, initially in conjunction with the Bank of England, and latterly with the FSA to provide regularly updated guidance on the various Money Laundering Regulations in force – those laid in 1993, 2001 and 2003.

THE RISK-BASED APPROACH

A major revision of JMLSG's Guidance was published in January 2006, based on a number of fundamental principles – including that of senior management accountability and the adoption of a risk-based approach. The risk-based approach allows firms to focus their money laundering deterrence and counter-terrorist financing resources on areas where the risk of money laundering and/or terrorist financing is considered highest. As we saw in Chapter 3, this had specifically been recommended by the Directive. The Guidance therefore embodies what are considered to be proportionate and cost-effective approaches to managing these risks.

A risk-based approach essentially includes the following:

- Senior management roles should include the identification of a Money Laundering Reporting Officer (or MLRO, see Chapter 9), responsible for the supervision of internal anti-money laundering policies, procedures and investigations, together with measures implemented to combat the financing of terrorism.

- Such policies and procedures must be formally documented. The documentation maintained must include a named employee as being responsible for implementing and assessing the risks faced by the firm.
- All firms must identify what they consider to be low risk and high risk clients. Low risk clients are normally seen as those with a regular income which have a long-term active relationship with the firm. High risk clients are generally the rest.

THE REGULATORY FRAMEWORK

The JMLSG has periodically reviewed its Guidance, and has made changes and additions as required. As mentioned above an important revision took place in 1993 to reflect the implementation of the Proceeds of Crime Act 2002 and there were then subsequent revisions that implemented the Money Laundering Regulations 2007, which in turn implemented the EU Third Money Laundering Directive in the UK.

The JMLSG states that the purpose of the Guidance is to:

- outline the legal and regulatory framework for money laundering deterrence and counter-terrorist financing requirements and systems across the UK financial services sector;
- interpret the requirements of the relevant law and regulations, and how they may be implemented in practice;
- indicate good industry practice in terms of money laundering deterrence and counter-terrorist financing procedures through a proportionate risk-based approach;
- assist firms to design and implement the systems and controls necessary to mitigate the risks of the firm being used in connection with money laundering and the financing of terrorism.

The actual Guidance is available for you to download for free from the following web site: www.jmlsg.com.

From this web site all of the rules can be seen in detail and they do form a useful reference set for money laundering deterrence specialists in any country. The Guidance is detailed and consistent with the FATF principles, together with relevant EU legislation, but actually goes much further in providing guidance in areas of specific concern. In the remainder of this book we do provide such guidance as is appropriate for the global reader. If you wish to look at specific UK guidance then reference does need to be made to the specific UK rules as set out on the above web site. Of course if you do require detailed local guidance then reference will need to be made to your local relevant authority and the rules that they have promulgated which achieve the same objectives.

Chapter 6

THE WOLFSBERG PRINCIPLES

THE WOLFSBERG GROUP

The Wolfsberg Group is a group of 11 financial institutions which aim to develop financial services industry standards and related policies for anti-money laundering and counter-terrorist financing. The 11 financial institutions consist of the following high profile international banks:

- Banco Santander
- Bank of Tokyo-Mitsubishi UF,
- Barclays
- Citigroup
- Credit Suisse
- Deutsche Bank
- Goldman Sachs
- HSBC
- JPMorgan
- Société Générale
- UBS.

The Group was formed in 2000, at the Château Wolfsberg in North-East Switzerland, to work on drafting anti-money laundering guidelines for private banking. The Wolfsberg anti-money laundering Principles for private banking were subsequently published in October 2000 (and were subsequently revised in May 2002).

What the group is seeking to achieve is in some ways similar to the objectives of the Financial Action Task Force as its main role is to support international efforts to combat corruption and anti-money laundering. However unlike other initiatives such as FATF (Chapter 2), which work closely with government agencies, the Wolfsberg Group is entirely led by the private sector. As a result, the Wolfsberg Group's numerous Principles, Guidelines and Statements are highly influential and generally considered as international best practice globally by industry regulators and the government bodies.

WHAT IS THE REAL SIGNIFICANCE OF THE PRINCIPLES?

In common with the FATF Principles and indeed the rules promulgated by the Bank for International Settlements, these Principles are also not in themselves legally binding in any country or on any institution. The idea is that they should be taken into consideration by regulators in the relevant industry in developing their rules. The variety and profile of financial institutions which make up the Wolfsberg Group does however give the group significant standing amongst regulators.

THE WOLFSBERG PRINCIPLES, STATEMENTS AND GUIDELINES

The Wolfsberg Group has issued guidelines, notices and statements on the following areas since its inception:

- Guidance on credit/charge card issuing and merchant acquiring activities – May 2009
- Trade finance principles – January 2009
- Wolfsberg Group, Clearing House Statement on Payment Message Standards – April 2007
- Notification for correspondent bank customers – April 2007
- Statement against corruption – February 2007
- Guidance on the risk-based approach for managing money laundering risks – March 2006
- Anti-money laundering guidance for mutual funds and other pooled investment vehicles – March 2006
- Statement on monitoring, screening and searching – September 2003
- Principles for correspondent banking – November 2002
- Statement on the suppression of the financing of terrorism – January 2002
- Principles on private banking – revised May 2002.

In the following sections we consider key elements of certain of these statements. Further information on individual elements of the statements appear in the relevant chapters of this book. If you do need full details of all or any of the statements, then reference should be made to the original statements themselves.

THE STATEMENT AGAINST CORRUPTION

The Statement generally defines corruption as the misuse of public office or public power for private gain by offering or promising anything of value – whether directly or indirectly – to a public official or a political candidate, party or party official, in order to obtain, retain or direct business or to secure any other improper advantage in the conduct of business. Notice that this is actually broader than the definition used by FATF as shown in Chapter 2. In this case the definition of corruption is clearly wider than the rather narrow definition of politically exposed person seen as a minimum by FATF.

Conversely, corruption involves the demanding or accepting of anything of value by such a person, as a condition to conferring business or other improper advantage whether directly or indirectly. Corruption is often associated with organised crime, money laundering and sometimes even the financing of terrorism. The problem with corruption is where does the provision of a service end and corruption begin? Paying a commission to an agent to assist in winning a contract is a normal business practice, indeed many agents receive the majority of their income from such sources.

The key point is that this is the nature of a disclosed business relationship, or a relationship which, were it to become public, would have no public interest issue related to it. Corruption is different – it suggests a payment to create advantage in a tender process. In the absence of paying the individual the firm would not win the contract. The corrupt official is now taking "commissions" in addition to their main employment and due to the nature of their position. The disclosure of such "commission" would cause public concern and would be considered inappropriate.

It is clear that the line between the two can become blurred and it is such issues which the Principles are seeking to address.

Generally combating corruption requires a comprehensive, multistakeholder approach which has to be led by supranational and national government agencies together with law enforcement, assisted by civil society and the wider business community.

Scope of the standard

The Statement addresses the issue of public corruption from the following key perspectives:

1. Internal measures which financial institutions may themselves consider to ensure that their own employees adhere to the high standards of integrity that are to be expected.
2. The misuse of financial institutions to further acts of corruption together with setting out some of the measures that financial

institutions could implement to attempt to mitigate their becoming inadvertently involved with corruption.

What internal measures are recommended?

This section of the Statement addresses the internal measures that financial institutions may consider taking to prevent their own employees and officers becoming involved in corruption.

Corruption is traditionally identified with the public sector, including public works, political parties, police, taxation and licensing authorities, and also with certain industrial sectors including defence, real estate, construction, oil and gas, and the metals and mining industries. A lot of corruption relates to government or municipality awarding of contracts, with a corrupt official being in a position to influence the selection process.

The Wolfsberg Group recommends that financial institutions consider appropriate measures which require their employees to adhere to high standards of integrity. In particular it states that financial institutions should prohibit the involvement of their own employees and officers in corruption in all business transactions carried out directly or indirectly when acting for or on behalf of their employer. What is considered to be an appropriate measure may include taking into account, for example, the size, nature and risks that a particular transaction or relationship would pose to the nature of each financial institution's business. In particular these could address:

- the offer and acceptance of gifts and controls on expenses related to travel and entertainment;
- the making of political and charitable contributions;
- the treatment of facilitation payments or commissions; and
- the use of intermediaries and/or agents, mandated on behalf of the financial institution.

The misuse of the financial system through corruption

The Principles identify that financial institutions may be misused, and in doing so further acts of corruption, in the following ways:

- a customer directing or collecting funds, for the purpose of paying a bribe;

- a recipient of a bribe placing illicit proceeds into the financial system;
- the deposit of misappropriated state assets; or
- the clearing of transactions in any of the above cases.

As you can see, the Principles set out that the financial institution could become involved with illegal activity at various stages of the process including layering and integration of proceeds.

The problem for the financial institution is that the transactions could appear to have a valid legal and also potentially a sound commercial basis. Without further information, it is difficult for the firm to make a distinction between accounts and transactions associated with corruption and those that are legally sound. This is particularly the case when dealing with substantial companies which have complex business operations and are generally involved with major international tenders and contracts. Ultimate responsibility to ensure that funds are neither collected nor used for illicit operations, including bribery, must clearly rest with a financial institution's customer or that customer's representatives. This needs to be recognised since a financial institution will seldom have a complete overview of its customer's financial activity, which is likely to involve a series of banks. Consequently the financial institution is likely to rely on its "know your customer" procedures to ensure that sufficient information is obtained to meet their requirements.

Transactions involving the proceeds of corruption often follow patterns of behaviour common to money laundering associated with other criminal activities; and adherence to existing anti-money laundering policies procedures and controls is therefore also important in the fight against corruption. This demonstrates that money laundering risks are closely related to corruption.

The risk-based approach

The Principles recognise that before applying relevant policies, procedures and controls financial institutions may consider it important to identify criteria to assess potential relevant risks throughout their respective business lines and areas of operation. A financial institution's general risk assessment methodology may include consideration of the following criteria:

- country risk
- customer risk

- industry risk
- transaction risk indicators ("red flags").

Where risk factors are identified, and a particular risk is of relevance to a customer, that should indicate that the transaction or customer would receive enhanced focus. Enhanced due diligence, transaction monitoring, senior management approval and additional monitoring oversight should all be applied to such customers and/or their financial operations as may be considered appropriate.

Suspicious activity reporting

Where a financial institution has reason to suspect corruption, further due diligence should be undertaken to ensure that there really is a suspicion. The completion of these further steps will lead to the prompt filing of a suspicious activity report with the appropriate authority.

THE STATEMENT ON PRIVATE BANKING (MAY 2002)

This Guideline provides a detailed overview for "know your client" (KYC) and Client Due Diligence (CDD), as well as providing rules for dealing with intermediaries.

Client acceptance

The Statement requires banks to endeavour to accept only those clients whose source of wealth and funds can be reasonably established to be legitimate. The responsibility to undertake this assessment lies with the private banker who sponsors the client for acceptance. In addition to the normal internal review procedures, the private banker should also consider the following factors.

Customer identification

The requirement is for reasonable measures to be undertaken to establish the identity of private banking clients and the beneficial owners of accounts. Generally banks should only accept clients when this process of identification has been completed. Another requirement is for identification documents that have been submitted to be current at the time of commencing the relationship.

Beneficial owner

Clearly beneficial ownership identification is key to understanding private banking relationships and consequently beneficial ownership must be established for all private banking accounts. Accordingly due diligence must be done on all principal beneficial owners identified in accordance with the following principles:

- **Natural persons** When the account is in the name of an individual, the client is acting on his/her own behalf. If doubt exists, the bank will establish the capacity in which and on whose behalf the account holder is acting.
- **Legal entities** Where the client is a company, such as a private investment company, the private banker will need to understand the structure of the company sufficiently to determine who is actually the provider of funds, who are the principal owner(s) of the shares and finally who actually has control over the funds.
- **Trusts** Where the client is a trust or a trustee, the private banker will need to understand the structure of the trust sufficiently to determine the provider of funds (e.g. settlor), those who have control over the funds (e.g. trustees) and any persons or entities who have the power to remove the trustees.
- **Accounts held in the name of money managers and similar intermediaries** In such cases the private banker should perform due diligence on the intermediary and establish that the intermediary also has a due diligence process for its clients, or a regulatory obligation to conduct such due diligence, that is considered as satisfactory to the bank.
- **Powers of attorney/Authorised signatories** Where the holder of a power of attorney or another authorised signatory is appointed by a client, it is generally sufficient for the private banker to undertake due diligence on the client. Unless there is some indication to the contrary there is no requirement to identify the person or firm holding the power of attorney.

Practices for walk-in clients and electronic banking relationships

The Statement requires that a bank should determine whether walk-in clients or relationships initiated through electronic channels require a higher degree of due diligence prior to account opening. The expectation is that banks will specifically address measures to satisfactorily establish the identity of non face-to-face customers which clearly represent a higher level of risk.

Due diligence

It is considered essential that a bank should collect and record information covering the following categories of activity:

- the purpose and reasons for opening the account;
- information on the anticipated account activity;
- the actual source of wealth or a description of the economic activity which has generated the net worth;
- the customer's estimated net worth;
- the actual source of funds, including a description of the origin and the means of transfer for monies that are accepted for the account opening;
- any references or other sources that have been used to corroborate reputation information, where available.

Unless other measures reasonably suffice to do the due diligence on a client (e.g. favourable and reliable references), the Statement requires that a client should generally be met prior to account opening.

It further states that numbered or alternative name accounts will only be accepted if the bank has already established the identity of the client and the beneficial owner. Such accounts must remain open to a level of additional scrutiny by the bank's appropriate control layers at least equal to the level of scrutiny applicable to other client accounts.

Client acceptance: situations requiring additional diligence/attention

The requirement here is that in its internal policies, the bank must define categories of persons whose circumstances warrant additional diligence. This will typically be the case where the circumstances indicate that the customer is likely to pose a higher than average risk to a bank.

The following categories of persons are set out as possible indicators for defining the subset of relationships which require additional diligence:

- Persons residing in and/or having funds sourced from countries identified by credible sources as having inadequate anti-money laundering standards or representing high risk for crime and corruption.
- Persons engaged in types of business activities or sectors known to be susceptible to money laundering.
- Politically exposed persons (PEPs), referring to individuals holding or having held positions of public trust, such as government officials, senior executives of government corporations, politicians, important political party officials, as well as their families and close associates.

PEPS are singled out for particular concerns with such relationships only being entered into with the approval from senior management.

Practices when identifying unusual or suspicious activities

The Statement requires a bank to have a written policy governing the identification of suspicious activities and the follow-up procedures that should be conducted. This policy should include a definition of what is considered to be a suspicious or unusual transaction and it should also provide examples.

Amongst a range of possible unusual or suspicious activities, the following are identified:

- account transactions or other activities which are not consistent with the information received on the customer during the due diligence process;
- cash transactions over a certain amount;
- pass-through /in-and-out-transactions, which appear to not have any real commercial intent.

The Statement notes that unusual or suspicious activities can be identified through:

- monitoring of transactions;
- client contacts;
- third party information;
- internal knowledge of the client's environment.

Monitoring

Clearly there is a requirement for an adequate monitoring programme to be in place. Here again there is the explicit requirement for the primary responsibility for monitoring account activity to lie with the private banker. This is because it is the private banker who will be sufficiently familiar with significant transactions and increased activity in the account and will therefore be especially aware of unusual or suspicious activities.

Education, training and information

There is a requirement that the bank should establish a training programme on the identification and prevention of money laundering for all employees who have client contact; and also for compliance personnel. Regular training (e.g. annually) will also need to include training on how to identify and follow up on unusual or suspicious activities. In addition, employees will need to be informed about any major changes in anti-money laundering laws and regulations which are relevant to their roles.

Generally there is a requirement that all new employees should be provided with guidelines on the anti-money laundering procedures implemented by the firm.

PRINCIPLES ON CORRESPONDENT BANKING

A separate Standard deals explicitly with correspondent banking, considering the nature of the reliance that can be placed on work conducted by such third party institutions.

Correspondent banking

Correspondent banking is defined as the provision of a current or other liability account and related services to another institution which is then used to meet its cash clearing, liquidity management and short-term borrowing or investment needs.

Risk-based due diligence

The Principles advocate that a firm should implement a risk-based approach in such cases, with clients presenting greater risk being subject to a higher level of due diligence. The Principles outline the type of risk indicators that an institution should consider when initiating the relationship, and also that they should review on a continuing basis, to ascertain what reasonable due diligence or enhanced due diligence should be undertaken. These include consideration of the following factors:

- **The client's domicile** This is the jurisdiction where the client is based, which may also reflect a level of additional risk when dealing with that bank or institution.
- **The client's ownership and management structures** The location of owners, their corporate legal form and the transparency of ownership structure may all represent greater risks. Similarly, the location and experience of management and the involvements of PEPs may raise additional concerns.
- **The client's business and customer base** The type of businesses the client engages in, as well as the type of the markets it serves, may represent greater risks. Higher risk clients are those clients that may be involved in activities or are connected to jurisdictions that are identified by credible sources as activities or countries being especially susceptible to money laundering.

Due diligence standards

Generally the requirement is for all clients to be subjected to appropriate due diligence procedures. In conducting such procedures, the elements set out below should be considered, as appropriate:

- **Client domicile and organisation** The bank should consider the jurisdiction where the client's ultimate parent is incorporated and/or headquartered and where the particular operating unit wishing to maintain the relationship conducts its business, as well as the corporate legal form of the client.
- **Client ownership and executive management** The institution should know whether the equity in the client is publicly held or privately owned, together with the identity of any significant controlling interests. There is a recommendation that the structure and experience of executive management should also be verified. The existence of any PEP in the executive management

or ownership structure would clearly represent a significant additional risk factor.

- **The client's business** The types of financial products and services that the client offers and the geographic markets supplied should also be identified.
- **Regulatory status and history** The primary regulatory body responsible for overseeing or supervising the client should be identified, together with whether the client has been the subject of any criminal or adverse regulatory action in the recent past.
- **Anti-money laundering controls** The nature of the client's anti-money laundering controls should be obtained, together with information related to the extent to which they are globally applied.
- **Shell banks** Generally there should be a requirement that the client will not use the institution's products and services to engage in business with shell banks. These are defined as banks that:
  - (i) do not conduct business at a fixed address in a jurisdiction in which the shell bank is authorised to engage in banking activities;
  - (ii) do not employ one or more individuals on a full-time business at this fixed address;
  - (iii) do not maintain operating records at this address; and
  - (iv) are not subject to inspection by the banking authority that licensed them to conduct banking activities.
- **Client visit** Unless other measures suffice, a representative of the financial institution should always visit the client at their premises prior to establishing a relationship with such a client.

Enhanced due diligence

In addition to normal due diligence, each institution will also subject those clients that represent greater risks to the firm to enhanced due diligence. This enhanced due diligence process will involve further consideration of key elements designed to ensure that the institution has secured a greater level of understanding of the client.

The key elements of the remaining Wolfsberg Principles have, where relevant, been included in the related chapters of this book.

Chapter 7

THE US REGULATORY FRAMEWORK

THE US PATRIOT ACT

The 342-page US Patriot Act forms the current cornerstone of US anti-money laundering deterrence legislation. Passed in 2001, the actual title of the legislation is:

Uniting and Strengthening America by Providing Appropriate Tools Required to Intercept and Obstruct Terrorism (USA PATRIOT ACT) Act of 2001.

As you will notice from the title the Patriot Act actually is not an "all crimes" piece of legislation and restricts itself to detecting and preventing terrorist financing only. Given the date that this legislation was passed by the House of Representatives (24 October 2001) this is perhaps not surprising, being signed by the then President, George Bush, on 26 October 2001.

This Act therefore adds to the existing US legislation on anti-money laundering by extending the Bank Secrecy Act across the entire financial services industry. However different institutions will find that the Act impacts them in different ways since there are additional criteria that relate to the size and complexity of an institution and the nature of their operations.

THE OTHER KEY US REGULATIONS

US banks were already subject to money laundering regulations prior to the enactment of this Act as shown in Table 7.1.

It is from the 1970 Bank Secrecy Act that the rules related to record retention and the requirement to report transactions of $10000+ emanate and these rules continue to apply. The 1986 Act introduced the key offences resulting from money laundering. Suspicious trans-

Table 7.1

Act	*Year*
Bank Secrecy Act	1970
Money Laundering Control Act	1986
Annunzio Wiley	1992
Money Laundering Suppression Act	1994
Funds Transfer Rules	1996

action reporting emanates from Annunzio Wiley, whereas suspicious activity reporting comes from the 1994 Money Laundering Suppression Act. Whilst you might hope that all of this regulation might be consolidated into a single Act, there is no suggestion that such consolidation is likely in the near future.

The US is the only country to have adopted such a piecemeal approach to money laundering deterrence and terrorist financing.

KEY ISSUES IN THE US PATRIOT ACT

As we have noted, the US Patriot Act is lengthy, perhaps too lengthy, and as discussed above it is predicated on the existing legislation. Its focus is on the requirements with respect to terrorist financing and therefore the obligations of the Patriot Act do not apply in respect of other offences.

This is to an extent a complication for the money laundering reporting officer (MLRO) operating in the US since the money laundering and terrorist financing rules, regulations and requirements will essentially be different. There are a lot of clauses, which relate to the role and authority of relevant agencies and courts to authorise or undertake surveillance or prosecution. These are not discussed here. However other clauses are of interest to financial institutions and are worthy of review.

Civil rights and safety

By putting safety as paramount the general stance of the Act is set within certain bounds which do differ from legislation enacted in other countries. Remember that reference will still need to be made to the Bank Secrecy Act in respect of other issues.

Asset seizure

Section 106 of the Patriot Act modifies provisions relating to presidential authority under the International Emergency Powers Act to authorise the President, when the United States is engaged in armed hostilities or has been attacked by a foreign country or foreign nationals, to confiscate any property subject to US jurisdiction of a foreign person, organisation, or country that he determines has planned, authorised, aided, or engaged in such hostilities or attacks.

This actually provides an interesting challenge for a firm. They clearly need to undertake enhanced due diligence in such cases and to provide data to agencies as required. The key question is whether such jurisdictions and nationals can be identified prior to their appearing on such a list to enable enhanced due diligence to take place. To some extent you would expect US banks to identify jurisdictions with which the US might become engaged in hostilities in advance – undertaking enhanced due diligence in all such cases.

What clearly is required is to know the jurisdiction of all customers, and this of course is required by general due diligence requirements.

Enhanced surveillance procedures

The clauses here amend the Federal Criminal Code to authorise the interception of wire, oral and electronic communications for the production of evidence of:

1. specified chemical weapons or terrorism offences; and
2. computer fraud and abuse.

Why are chemical weapons specifically referred to and not, for example, nuclear weapons? Again this really relates to the way in which the legislation was enacted. The rules set out the way in which the authorities can legally undertake investigation procedures and also set out the various extraterritorial implications. Interestingly the legislation permits the seizure of voicemail messages under a warrant.

They also expand the scope of subpoenas for records of electronic communications to include the length and types of service utilised, temporarily assigned network addresses, and the means and source of payment (including any credit card or bank account number).

In terms of the logistical issues, there is a statement that nothing in the Act shall impose any additional technical obligation or requirement on a provider of a wire or electronic communication service or other person to furnish facilities or technical assistance. Further a provider of this type of service, and a landlord, custodian, or other person who furnishes these facilities or technical assistance, shall be reasonably compensated for such reasonable expenditure incurred in providing such facilities or assistance.

This means that there is nothing additional that such firms are required to do – but if they are required to do anything then they will in principle be adequately compensated. In this the regulations do not actually go as far as the regulations implemented in other countries where they are requiring electronic communication service providers to maintain records for a specified time period to facilitate investigations that might be required. Whether there is any real compensation is of course another matter.

International counter money laundering and related measures

This part of the Patriot Act amends Federal law governing monetary transactions to prescribe procedural guidelines under which the Secretary of the Treasury (the Secretary) may require domestic financial institutions and agencies to take specified measures if the Secretary finds that reasonable grounds exist for concluding that jurisdictions, financial institutions, types of accounts, or transactions operating outside or within the United States, are of primary money laundering concern. The requirements include mandatory disclosure of specified information relating to certain correspondent accounts. It is these sections which actually impose the greatest burden on a financial institution.

The Act mandates the establishment of due diligence mechanisms to detect and report money laundering transactions through private banking accounts and correspondent accounts, issues already dealt with by the Wolfsberg Principles (Chapter 6). The Act makes these Principles mandatory with the obligation on detection and subsequent reporting, although this is in relation only to terrorist financing.

The systems that will be implemented in practice clearly fall into two categories – those systems that look for specific attributes (or scenarios) and those that look for unusual transactions (based on some system-defined inference process). Given the level of data that is maintained by a financial institution, most financial institutions will implement software to assist such suspicion recognition. This is further considered in Chapter 23.

The Act prohibits US banks maintaining correspondent accounts with foreign shell banks, one of the Financial Actions Task Force (FATF) requirements which also appears within the Wolfsberg Principles.

Extra territorial arrangements can become a problem, since the Act establishes Federal jurisdiction over:

1. foreign money launderers (including their assets held in the United States); and
2. money that is laundered through a foreign bank.

Forfeiture rules

Section 319 authorises the forfeiture of money laundering funds from interbank accounts. It also requires that a financial institution, upon request of the appropriate Federal banking agency, to make available within 120 hours all pertinent information related to anti-money laundering compliance by the institution or its customer.

Firms need to have regard to this 120-hour rule and ensure that their systems have the capability to provide information in the form required on a timely basis.

It further grants the Secretary summons and subpoena powers over foreign banks that maintain a correspondent bank in the United States. Finally there is also a requirement that a financial institution subject to these rules must terminate within 10 business days any correspondent relationship with a foreign bank after receipt of written notice that the foreign bank has failed to comply with certain judicial proceedings, together with setting out the civil penalties for failure to terminate such relationship.

Clearly correspondent banking relationships should be under regular review such that the firm can satisfy itself that it is being operated in accordance with international best practice and local jurisdictional regulation.

Identification, record and reporting requirements

The record and reporting requirements appear within Section 321 of the Act. It subjects to record and report requirements for monetary instrument transactions:

1. any credit union; and
2. any futures commission merchant, commodity trading advisor, and commodity pool operator registered, or required to register, under the Commodity Exchange Act.

Section 325 then authorises the Secretary to issue regulations to ensure that concentration accounts of financial institutions are not used to prevent association of the identity of an individual customer with the movement of funds of which the customer is the direct or beneficial owner, whilst Section 326 directs the Secretary to issue regulations prescribing minimum standards for financial institutions regarding customer identity in connection with the opening of accounts

Bank Holding Company Act

Section 327 amends the Bank Holding Company Act of 1956 and the Federal Deposit Insurance Act to require consideration of the effectiveness of a company or companies in combating money laundering during reviews of proposed bank shares acquisitions or mergers.

Section 328 then implements another of the FATF special recommendations by directing the Secretary to take reasonable steps to encourage foreign governments to require the inclusion of the name of the originator in wire transfer instructions sent to the United States and other countries, with the information to remain with the transfer from its origination until the point of disbursement.

Bank Secrecy Act amendments and related improvements

The Act also amends the Bank Secrecy Act (BSA) to revise requirements for civil liability immunity for voluntary financial institution disclosure of suspicious activities. It authorises the inclusion of suspicions of illegal activity in written employment references.

Section 356 instructs the Secretary to:

1. promulgate regulations requiring registered securities brokers and dealers, futures commission merchants, commodity trading advisors and commodity pool operators, to file reports of suspicious financial transactions;
2. report to Congress on the role of the Internal Revenue Service in the administration of the Bank Secrecy Act; and
3. share monetary instruments transactions records upon request of a US intelligence agency for use in the conduct of intelligence or counterintelligence activities, including analysis, to protect against international terrorism.

Section 359 extends the requirements to cover any licensed sender of money or any other person who engages as a business in the transmission of funds, including through an informal value transfer banking system or network (e.g., hawala).

Penalties

The Act also increases the penalties that may be levied in respect of terrorist financing. Section 363 increases to $1 million the maximum civil penalties (from the rather dated $10 000) and criminal fines (currently $250 000) for money laundering. It also sets a minimum civil penalty and criminal fine of double the amount of the illegal transaction. Section 365 amends Federal law to require reports relating to coins and currency of more than $10 000 received in a nonfinancial trade or business.

Currency crimes

The Act also establishes a bulk cash smuggling felony of the knowing concealment and attempted transport (or transfer) across US borders of currency and monetary instruments in excess of $10 000, with intent to evade specified currency reporting requirements.

Further extraterritorial requirements sit in Section 377. This section grants the United States extraterritorial jurisdiction where:

1. an offence committed outside the United States involves an access device issued, owned, managed or controlled by a financial institution, account issuer, credit card system member or other entity within US jurisdiction; and
2. the person committing the offence transports, delivers, conveys, transfers to or through, or otherwise stores, secretes, or holds within US jurisdiction any article used to assist in the commission of the offence or the proceeds of such offence or property derived from it.

Strengthening the criminal laws against terrorism

The Act also amends the Federal criminal code to prohibit specific terrorist acts or otherwise destructive, disruptive or violent acts against mass transportation vehicles, ferries, providers, employees, passengers, or operating systems. Section 803 prohibits harbouring any person knowing or having reasonable grounds to believe that such person has committed or is about to commit a terrorism offence, whilst Section 804 establishes Federal jurisdiction over crimes committed at US facilities abroad.

THE BANK SECRECY ACT 1970

The Currency and Foreign Transactions Reporting Act, also known as the Bank Secrecy Act (BSA), and its implementing regulation, 31 CFR 103, is a tool the US government uses to fight drug trafficking, money laundering and other crimes. Congress enacted the BSA to prevent banks and other financial service providers from being used as intermediaries for, or to hide the transfer or deposit of money derived from, criminal activity. The Office of the Comptroller of the Currency (OCC) monitors national bank compliance with the BSA and 31 CFR 103.

More than 170 crimes are listed in the federal money laundering statutes. They range from drug trafficking, gunrunning, murder for hire, fraud, acts of terrorism and the illegal use of wetlands. The list also includes certain foreign crimes. Therefore, a financial institution must educate its employees, understand its customers and their businesses, and have systems and procedures in place to distinguish routine transactions from ones that rise to the level of suspicious activity.

US penalties for money laundering can be severe. Individuals, including bank employees, convicted of money laundering face up to 20 years in prison for each money laundering transaction. Businesses, including banks and individuals, face fines up to the greater of $500 000 or twice the value of the transaction. Any property involved in the transaction or traceable to the proceeds of the criminal activity, including loan collateral, personal property and, under certain conditions, entire bank accounts (even if some of the money in the account is legitimate) may be subject to forfeiture. In addition, banks risk losing their charter, and bank employees risk being removed and barred from banking.

Under the provisions of the Controlled Substances Act of 1978, the Money Laundering Control Act of 1986, and the Anti-Drug Abuse Act of 1988, real or personal property traceable to illegal drug sales or purchased with laundered money is subject to government seizure and forfeiture. Occasionally, seized property is collateral for bank loans. Therefore, a bank must obtain and confirm enough information about its customers to protect its loan collateral from loss due to government forfeiture.

Independent testing of compliance

The bank's internal or external auditors should be able to:

- attest to the overall integrity and effectiveness of management systems and controls, and BSA technical compliance;
- test transactions in all areas of the bank with emphasis on high risk areas, products, and services to ensure the bank is following prescribed regulations;
- assess employees' knowledge of regulations and procedures;
- assess adequacy, accuracy, and completeness of training programmes;
- assess adequacy of the bank's process for identifying suspicious activity.

Internal review or audit findings should be incorporated into a board and senior management report and reviewed promptly. There then needs to be appropriate follow-up.

Compliance officer

A national bank must designate a qualified bank employee as its BSA compliance officer, who has day-to-day responsibility for managing all aspects of the BSA compliance programme and compliance with all BSA Regulations. The BSA compliance officer may delegate certain BSA compliance duties to other employees, but not compliance responsibility.

The bank's board of directors and senior management must ensure that the BSA compliance officer has sufficient authority and resources to administer effectively a comprehensive BSA compliance programme.

Training

Banks must ensure that appropriate bank personnel are trained in all aspects of the regulatory requirements of the BSA and the bank's internal BSA compliance and anti-money laundering policies and procedures. An effective training programme includes provisions to ensure that all bank personnel, including senior management, who have contact with customers (whether in person or by phone), who see customer transaction activity or who handle cash in any way, receive appropriate training.

Those employees include persons involved with branch administration; customer service; lending, private, or personal banking; correspondent banking (international and domestic); trust; discount brokerage; funds transfer; safe deposit/custody; and vault activities.

Training is ongoing and incorporates current developments and changes to relevant regulations. New and different types of money laundering schemes that have evolved in the market and might involve customers and financial institutions should be addressed. It also should include examples of money laundering schemes and cases, tailored to the audience, and the ways in which such activities can be detected or resolved.

Training focuses on the consequences of an employee's failure to comply with established policy and procedures (e.g., fines or termination). Programmes should provide personnel with guidance and direction in terms of bank policies and available resources.

Reporting requirements

The BSA Regulations require all financial institutions to submit five types of reports to the government.

1. **IRS Form 4789 Currency Transaction Report (CTR)** A CTR must be filed for each deposit, withdrawal, exchange of currency, or other payment or transfer, by, through or to a financial institution, which involves a transaction in currency of *more than* \$10 000. Multiple currency transactions must be treated as a single transaction if the financial institution *has knowledge* that: (a) they are conducted by or on behalf of the same person; and, (b) they result in cash received or disbursed by the financial institution of more than \$10 000. (31 CFR 103.22)

2. **US Customs Form 4790 Report of International Transportation of Currency or Monetary Instruments (CMIR)** Each person (including a bank) who physically transports, mails or ships, or causes to be physically transported, mailed, shipped or received, currency, traveller's cheques and certain other monetary instruments in an

aggregate amount *exceeding* $10 000 into or out of the United States must file a CMIR. (31 CFR 103.23)

3. Department of the Treasury Form 90-22.1 Report of Foreign Bank and Financial Accounts (FBAR) Each person (including a bank) subject to the jurisdiction of the United States having an interest in, signature or other authority over, one or more bank, securities, or other financial accounts in a foreign country must file an FBAR if the aggregate value of such accounts at any point in a calendar year *exceeds* $10 000. (31 CFR 103.24)

4. Treasury Department Form 90-22.47 and OCC Form 8010-9, 8010-1 Suspicious Activity Report (SAR) Banks must file a SAR for any suspicious transaction relevant to a possible violation of law or regulation. (31 CFR 103.18) (12 CFR 12.11)

5. "Designation of Exempt Person" Form TDF 90-22.53 Banks must file this form to designate an exempt customer for the purpose of CTR reporting under the BSA (31 CFR 103.22(d)(3)(i)). In addition, banks use this form biennially (every two years) to renew exemptions for eligible nonlisted business and payroll customers. (31 CFR 103.22(d)(5)(i))

Record-keeping requirements

The BSA Regulations require banks to maintain a variety of records to ensure, among other things, that transactions can be reconstructed. Two of those record-keeping requirements are discussed below. Detailed descriptions of these and other record-keeping requirements for banks can be found in 31 CFR 103. The retention period for all records required to be kept under the BSA Regulations is five years.

1. Monetary Instrument Sales Records A bank must retain a record of each *cash* sale of bank cheques, drafts, cashier's cheques, money orders, and traveller's cheques between $3000 and $10 000 inclusive. These records must include evidence of verification of the identity of the purchaser and other information. (31 CFR 103.29)

2. Funds Transfer Record Keeping and Travel Rule Requirements A bank must maintain a record of each funds transfer of $3000 or more which it originates, acts as an intermediary for, or receives. The amount and type of information a bank must record and keep depends upon its role in the funds transfer process. Also, a bank that acts as an originator or intermediary for a funds transfer must pass certain information along to the next bank in the funds transfer chain. (31 CFR 103.33 (e) and (g))

Under the phase II rule 12 months of account history must exist before the customer can be exempted. (The months do not have to be consecutive, but should be recent.)

- The customer must engage frequently in large currency transactions (eight or more a year).
- The customer must be incorporated or organised under the laws of the United States or a state, or registered or eligible to do business in the United States.
- Annually, banks must verify whether each exemption continues to meet the exemption eligibility requirements. Banks may develop their own methods and procedures for this annual review.
- Biennially, banks must file the "Designation of Exempt Person" form for each nonlisted business and payroll customer.
- As part of the biennial filing of the "Designation of Exempt Person" form, the bank must certify that, as part of its BSA compliance programme, it has policies and procedures in place for identifying, reviewing, and reporting suspicious activity in accordance with the SAR filing requirements. (31 CFR 103.18 and 12 CFR 21.11)

Suspicious activity reporting requirements

An effective BSA compliance programme includes controls and measures to identify and timely report suspicious transactions. A financial institution must apply due diligence to be able to make an informed decision about the suspicious nature of a particular transaction and whether to file a suspicious activity report (SAR). SARs must be filed within prescribed time frames following the discovery of:

- insider abuse involving any amount;
- violations of federal law aggregating $5000 or more when a suspect can be identified;
- violations of federal law aggregating $25 000 or more regardless of a potential suspect;
- transactions aggregating $5000 or more that involve potential money laundering or violations of the BSA if the bank knows, suspects or has reason to suspect that the transaction:
    - involves funds from illegal activities or is intended or conducted to hide or disguise illicit funds or assets as part of a

plan to violate or evade any law or regulation or to avoid any transaction reporting requirement under federal law;

- is designed to evade any of the BSA Regulations; or
- has no business or apparent lawful purpose or is not the sort in which the particular customer would normally be expected to engage, and the bank knows of no reasonable explanation for the transaction after examining the available facts, including the background and possible purpose of the transaction.

The rules continue to provide additional guidance regarding the identification of potential money laundering, repeating much of the material already included within this Handbook.

Chapter 8

FINANCIAL SANCTIONS

WHAT ARE FINANCIAL SANCTIONS?

Financial sanctions are orders which prevent firms from dealing with individuals or organisations who can be linked to the financing of terrorism. Individuals or organisations linked with the financing of terrorism or nuclear proliferation are also known as "targets". This is an approach which operates within the international community through the provision of lists, as well as through individual governments acting unilaterally. For example, it is an offence under UK law to provide funds to those on the international list, unless in the case of financial institutions, a licence is obtained from Her Majesty's Treasury. Financial sanctions are mostly international targets, and currently there are around 50 UK individuals and entities on the HM Treasury sanctions lists.

FAILING TO COMPLY

Firms which allow individuals connected with financing terrorism to maintain accounts or undertake transactions with them risk criminal penalties. In this case the penalties would be enforced by the government against the firm, and in some cases also against the management directly. The legal consequences of failing to comply with the orders can be substantial. In the US, the US Dept of Justice levied fines on Lloyds of $350 million for breaches of US sanctions against Iran and Sudan on 9 January 2009. This was at that time the largest-ever penalty under US sanctions legislation.

The Department of Justice press release stated:

> Under the IEEPA, it is a crime to willfully violate, or attempt to violate, any regulation issued under the act, including the Iranian Transactions Regulations, which prohibit exportation of services from the United States to Iran, and the Sudanese Sanctions Regulations, which prohibit exportation of services from the United States to Sudan.
>
> According to court documents, beginning as early as 1995 and continuing until January 2007, Lloyds, in both the United Kingdom and Dubai, falsified outgoing U.S. wire transfers that involved countries or persons on U.S. sanctions lists. Specifically, according to court documents, Lloyds deliberately removed material information – such

as customer names, bank names and addresses – from payment messages so that the wire transfers would pass undetected through filters at U.S. financial institutions. This process of "repairing" or "stripping," as Lloyds commonly referred to it, allowed more than $350 million in transactions to be processed by U.S. correspondent banks used by Lloyds that might have otherwise been blocked or rejected due to sanctions regulations or for internal bank policy reasons. According to court documents, the criminal conduct by Lloyds was designed to evade, and to assist its customers in evading, U.S. economic sanctions imposed against Iran, Sudan and other countries.

"For more than 12 years, Lloyds facilitated the anonymous movement of hundreds of millions of dollars from U.S.-sanctioned nations through our financial system," said Acting Assistant Attorney General Matthew Friedrich. "More than $350 million moved from places such as Iran through locations around the world because Lloyds stripped identifying information from international wire transfers that would have raised a red flag at U.S. financial institutions and caused such payments to be scrutinized. The Department will continue to use criminal enforcement measures against the knowing and intentional evasion of U.S. sanctions laws, particularly where such conduct has the potential to finance terrorist activities."

The bank's forfeiture of $175 million to the United States and $175 million to New York County settled forfeiture claims by the Department of Justice and the State of New York.

Aside from the financial penalties for firms, the reputational risk that a firm will suffer from being associated with the funding of terrorism will potentially be immense. Clearly therefore the firm needs to implement full and complete policies, process, procedures and training to alert staff to the issues and involved and minimise the risks as far as is possible.

SANCTIONS LISTS

Lists of targets, which firms must avoid dealings with, can be found at HM Treasury's web site at http://www.hm-treasury.gov.uk/d/sanctionsconlist.pdf

For each organisation listed specific details of individuals associated with the organisation are set out in reasonable detail, the following being an example:

108. **Name 6:** BIN LADEN **1:** USAMA **2:** MUHAMMED **3:** AWAD **4:** n/a **5:** n/a. **Title:** Shaykh/Hajj **DOB:** (1) 28/07/1957. (2) 30/07/1957. (3) 10/03/1957. (4) 01/01/1957. (5) -/-/1956. (6) -/-/1957. **POB:** (1) - (2) Jeddah, (1) Yemen (2) Saudi Arabia **a.k.a:** (1) ABD AL-HAKIM, Abu Abdallah (2) AL QAQA (3) AWDH, Bin Laden, Osama, Mohamed (4) BIN LADEN, Usama (5) BIN LADIN, Shaykh, Usama (6) BIN LADIN, Usamah, Bin Muhammad (7) BIN MUHAMMAD, Bin Laden, Usamah (8) OSAMA, Ben Laden (9) OSSAMA, Ben Laden (10) USAMA, Ben Laden (11) USAMA BIN MUHAMMED BIN AWAD, Osama Bin Laden **Nationality:** Saudi citizenship withdrawn. Now officially an Afghan national **Other Information:** UN Ref QI.B.8.01 **Listed on:** 23/02/2001 **Last Updated:** 09/07/2007 **Group ID:** 6896.

The list literally goes from A to Z over 109 pages, or from Al-Qaida to:

40. **Organisation Name:** ZIMRE REINSURANCE COMPANY (PVT) LIMITED **Address:** 9th Floor, Zimre Centre, 25 Kwama Nkrumah Avenue, Harare, Zimbabwe. **Other Information:** Wholly owned by Zimre Holdings Limited. **Listed on:** 27/01/2009 **Last Updated:** 27/01/2009 **Group ID:** 10830.

So the list does include both well known and not so well known organisations.

The current list of inappropriate regimes set out on the web site is as follows:

- Al-Qaida and Taliban
- Belarus
- Burma/Myanmar
- Democratic Republic of Congo
- Federal Republic of Yugoslavia & Serbia
- International Criminal Tribunal for The Former Yugoslavia
- Iran
- Iraq
- Ivory Coast
- Lebanon and Syria
- Liberia
- North Korea (Democratic People's Republic of Korea)
- Sudan

- Terrorism and terrorist financing
- Zimbabwe.

The Asset Freezing Unit in the Treasury is responsible for the implementation and administration of international financial sanctions in effect in the UK, for domestic designations principally under the Terrorism Order (Terrorism (U.N. Measures) Order and the Al-Qaida and Taliban (U.N. Measures) Order 2006. In the event that a customer is found to be on a financial sanctions list, the obligation is on the firm to immediately stop providing services or products to the target and to then contact HM Treasury's Asset Freezing Unit.

These UK lists will potentially prove of assistance to any firms in designing procedures to identify what might be considered as the highest risk customers. Of course such firms, organisations and individuals regularly change their identities and so the historic nature of such information must always be a concern to a firm. However any financial institution would be expected to have identified and acted upon what is in effect a public analysis of areas of concern. When this is combined with the information promulgated by Transparency International it will prove to be of assistance if a firm is undertaking scenario modelling or is in the process of developing a risk-based approach.

COMPLIANCE WITH FINANCIAL SANCTIONS

Firms must ensure that they develop policies and procedures to ensure compliance with local financial sanctions legislation and guidance. In order to ensure compliance with financial sanctions regulations, the following actions are recommended:

- A firm should undertake and regularly review risk assessments, especially on clients involved in either the weapons or components industries, together with market counterparties from certain specified higher risk jurisdictions.
- A firm should also establish and regularly review a clear counter-terrorist financing policy which has been tailored to their business profile.
- They should clearly develop appropriate operating procedures which should be regularly reviewed and amended to ensure that

they remain appropriate for the firm and be consistent with the policies and goals of the firm.

- Financial sanctions awareness and the importance of these rules should be included within training and awareness programmes for all staff to enable them to understand both their personal and their corporate obligations.
- Specific additional procedures should be implemented to address new and transferred clients or counterparties where these originate from high risk countries.
- Generally firms should evaluate the source and origin of funds, together with country risk leading to identification of high priority relationships that should be subject to enhanced due diligence and monitoring as part of the implementation of the risk-based approach.

FINANCIAL SANCTIONS AS PART OF NORMAL MONEY LAUNDERING DETERRENCE PROCEDURES

In many firms financial sanctions are not currently checked as part of the existing anti-money laundering procedures implemented as part of a general deterrence regime. Unlike the risk-based processes and procedures which are generally appropriate for money laundering deterrence, the financial sanctions rules are different. In this case the financial sanctions must be checked when carrying out any transaction and this is not dependant on the threshold amount of the transaction concerned. It is the nature of the transaction which breaches the rules, not its size.

Furthermore, whilst politically exposed persons form part of money laundering deterrence regulation, that monitoring should not be considered as being similar to monitoring for compliance with financial sanctions. The main difference here is that a PEP is classified as anyone who holds or is associated with a high profile political position as discussed in Chapter 14. Being a PEP does not mean the person is guilty of money laundering or other illegal activity, rather it implies that enhanced due diligence should be conducted.

Financial sanctions are usually targets known in the world of financial crime because of their illegal activities which include the financing of terrorism and nuclear proliferation. As such, targets on these lists are aware that they are on a sanctions list, which is public. Since this is therefore public information there can be no equivalent offence of "tipping off". The regulated firm needs to know whether they are dealing with such people and act accordingly – there is no choice in such cases.

DIFFICULTIES FACED BY FIRMS WHEN MONITORING FINANCIAL SANCTIONS

Firms who fail to have in place procedures, systems and controls to monitor financial sanctions can face heavy financial penalties as a result of either misconceptions and a general lack of understanding exhibited by their staff. It is vital for firms to remember that financial sanctions require additional attention, and are not monitored as part of general money laundering deterrence systems and controls. Some of the common misconceptions which firms have regarding financial sanctions are summarised below:

1. It is important to remember that financial sanctions apply to all firms, and not just banks or financial institutions.
2. Firms also have a common misconception that if they process only low value transactions they are not subject to financial sanctions requirements. Remember that the targets on financial sanctions lists are on those lists irrespective of any financial limits.
3. There is a wide range of targets typically on such lists. In the UK the list includes both UK-based targets as well as international targets. A UK firm for example cannot assume that all targets are only UK-based.
4. Financial sanctions regulations will apply to firms even if they do not hold client money.
5. The offence of tipping off is not an issue since those on the sanctions list already know they are on the list, so at least that is one thing that does not need to be worried about.
6. Politically exposed persons (or PEPs) are not the same as sanctions targets but some PEPs may also be on the sanctions list.
7. Financial sanctions regulations also apply to insurance companies.
8. Typical money laundering deterrence due diligence monitoring requirements are not the same as sanctions list screening, but they may be closely linked.

9. Sanctions compliance is a completely discrete legal regime and does not adopt a risk-based approach.
10. Sanctions checks carried out by third parties can only be relied on when the accepting firm has verified that the referring firm has completed recent sanctions screening.

So for a firm operating in any jurisdiction, the obligation is to understand and comply with their local financial sanctions both in their home country and in any host countries where they operate branches or subsidiaries. In most countries ignorance of the fact that a person is on the sanctions list is not sufficient to avoid prosecution for the offence of assisting terrorist financing.

Chapter 9

THE ROLE OF THE MONEY LAUNDERING REPORTING OFFICER

WHAT IS A MONEY LAUNDERING REPORTING OFFICER?

Global money laundering regulations place responsibilities, accountabilities and procedures on individual countries to prevent and detect money laundering activity. In order to comply with the systems and control function firms are generally required to appoint a responsible individual to take ownership of the process, normally referred to as a Money Laundering Reporting Officer (or MLRO).

The MLRO should be the first point of contact within a firm for any issues which relate directly or indirectly to money laundering deterrence or suspected terrorist financing activity. They should be responsible for any strategic decisions concerning money laundering and financial crime. The MLRO therefore has ultimate managerial responsibility for regulation of money laundering; insufficient performance of this role can result in fines being issued by the appropriate regulatory authority, depending on the rules of the relevant jurisdiction.

WHO CAN BE APPOINTED AS AN MLRO?

An MLRO will normally hold a senior management position, and will be trained on regulatory and compliance issues concerning money laundering deterrence and terrorist financing. A relevant firm should generally appoint an MLRO who has a sufficient level of seniority within the firm. Clearly the MLRO must also have sufficient resources, time and support staff to enable them to undertake their role effectively. The duty normally sits with the firm to ensure that MLRO is able to monitor the day-to-day operation of its money laundering and terrorist financing deterrence activities. The MLRO must also be able to respond promptly to any reasonable request for information made by relevant regulatory authorities.

The question then arises whether the role of the MLRO can easily be combined with another role within the firm. This is particularly an issue for the smaller firm. Combining the role of the MLRO with that of the compliance officer, who takes responsibility for ensuring that the business complies with all other rules and regulations, can be considered as an appropriate solution. No other role actually provides the same level of independence that is required and combination with the role of Head of Internal Audit would not appear to be ideal. Since internal audit reports essentially to the Audit Committee and undertakes work at their behest, they will also wish to conduct audits into the money laundering and terrorist financing deterrence procedures that have been implemented within the firm.

If another role is to be combined with that of the MLRO, then the key issue to consider is to what extent is the role either client or counterparty facing, or able to influence the recording or processing of such transactions. If any role does exist without any of these responsibilities, then this may become the least bad alternative.

THE ROLE OF THE MLRO

The MLRO is responsible for the overseeing of implementation of anti-money laundering and terrorist financing deterrence strategies and policies.

The key elements of the MLRO role will usually consist of:

- making strategic decisions concerning suspicious activity reports;
- responsibility to deal with internal reporting of suspicious activity;
- responsibility to report to and send notifications and disclosures to the appropriate regulatory authorities. In the UK this role is currently undertaken by the Serious Organised Crime Agency (SOCA);
- establishing and maintaining arrangements for awareness and training to all internal staff;
- monitoring and controlling money laundering policies and procedures;
- producing an annual report covering the anti-money laundering activity of the previous year;
- liaising with regulatory authorities to deal with such matters as consent to proceed with a transaction and other disclosure issues, particularly with regards to clients or third parties.

One of the key elements resulting in the appointment of the MLRO is the protection normally afforded to them through locally implemented legislation. It is such legislation that protects the MLRO and enables them to override customer confidentiality in making reports to the relevant reporting agency. Such protection does not normally extend to any other parties within the regulated entity. The MLRO is also normally able to undertake their investigations, leading to a conclusion as to whether a case will or will not be reported, knowing that in the absence of manifest negligence they will actually also be protected.

Clearly the exact legal protections afforded by local legislation will vary and again reference should be made to local rules where detailed guidance is required.

THE SAFE HARBOUR AND ITS LIMITATIONS

Global money laundering regulations specify that any MLRO acting less than diligently will still be subject to certain sanctions. The extent of such a sanction will vary depending on the relevant regulation that has been implemented locally. There will generally be a defence within most money laundering regulations to act as a safe harbour for the MLRO in respect of any action resulting from breaching data secrecy and confidentiality rules, as long as they act diligently. The typical wording of most regulations will state that the MLRO still needs to have demonstrated that they have maintained due care and attention in order to obtain protection from prosecution. To achieve this there is clearly an obligation on the MLRO to maintain adequate documentation to support the decisions that they have made.

Again the maintenance of detailed policies and procedures together with relevant documentation is always the best way for the MLRO to demonstrate that they have acted appropriately; so long as they are clearly complied with. To make sure that such processes and procedures are adequate many MLROs will have their documentation reviewed by internationally recognised legal experts to confirm their compliance with best practice and local regulation.

MATRIX MANAGEMENT

One of the MLRO's main roles is the reporting of suspicious activity and ensuring that sufficient procedures are in place to carry out the required reporting to the relevant authority. In some cases the MLRO may delegate some of its role to a deputy MLRO. Generally speaking, it is not advisable to have too many people involved in the process of reporting suspicions, as the required confidentiality of the process may be compromised. The more direct the process of reporting a suspicion is, the less likely the risk of the client being alerted to a suspicion.

In large corporations, the sheer volume of suspicions which an MLRO receives means it will not always be practical for the MLRO to have sole responsibility for receiving notifications and suspicions. Therefore larger, more complex corporations will have a system of dual notification in place whereby notifications of suspicions can be reported to either the MLRO or another individual within the business unit. Such a role is generally separate from the role that a deputy MLRO may have delegated to them. The idea is to have an alternative contact within the firm, who has a high level of training, but operates in a different part of the business structure. This type of role tends to be allocated to compliance officers. Compliance officers have a quasi-legal background and so they are able to contribute a high level of knowledge and expertise to the process.

However the main criterion to have in mind when allocating this role is to appoint someone whose role is as little client facing as possible. The reasoning behind this is that limited client contact means the reporting officer is less likely to inadvertently alert clients to any suspicions. Once a suspicion has been raised it is usually difficult for an employee who has knowledge of such reporting and deals directly with the reported client to remain independent and avoid instigating probing questions from a potentially wary client. For example, a client relationship manager who deals with a client under suspicion may need to continuously find reasons to delay completing a transaction which involves transferring funds. The client will clearly be alerted to the possibility of concerns if the client relationship manager is now suddenly always unavailable. There is also the possibility that employees who work closely with their clients may in rare cases themselves be involved in the fraud or money laundering. It is therefore advisable to maintain a degree of separation in order to dilute the degree of influence which such an employee might have.

While we have outlined the benefits of appointing an alternative notifying officer from a higher, non client facing level, we realise that this style of structure may be primarily limited to large corporations. Employees of small companies tend to have an overlap in functions and responsibilities, with it being possible that all functions may in some sense be client facing. This may be addressed with the possibility of outsourcing some of the work of the MLRO, whilst not outsourcing the legal responsibilities. This clearly will help maintain an MLRO's independence and, as an outsourced resource will certainly not have any contact with clients, maintains confidentiality.

WHAT IS AN MLRO'S INTERNAL REPORTING PROCEDURE?

All suspicions identified within the business must be reported to the MLRO or to a deputy MLRO, if the MLRO has chosen to appoint one. Ideally the process of reporting suspicions should be as direct and timely as possible. All suspicions which are reported to the MLRO should be fully documented, with the date and time together with the full name of the member of staff and position and role within the firm recorded.

An initial report should be prepared with details of the customer and a full statement detailing information giving rise to the suspicion. The MLRO will then acknowledge receipt of the report and inform the member of staff to do nothing which may prejudice any potential investigation or tip off the customer. All internal enquiries, including investigations conducted to confirm the suspicion and decisions made as to whether or not to submit the report to the relevant reporting agency, should also be fully documented.

This is done as a matter of good practice to enable the MLRO to make reference to past suspicions, should an investigation subsequently arise, and to provide some level of defence in case of reports not made after investigation, highlighting that appropriate actions were in fact taken. Reports should also include whether any transactions were actually prevented from proceeding any further as a result of a money laundering suspicion being identified.

It is also good practice for the MLRO to maintain a register of suspicions received, investigated and reported to provide some monitoring of the process. This will in particular highlight any cases where the MLRO has been required by the relevant agency to take specific action, such as freezing an account. It will also highlight the number of cases where the MLRO has made a report, but there has been no direct response from the relevant agency of any kind.

WHAT IS CONTAINED IN THE MLRO'S ANNUAL REPORT?

In order to maintain adequate systems and controls for compliance with its regulatory obligations, in many countries firms are required to commission an annual report from their MLRO. Such an annual report aims to focus on specific outcomes rather than to just provide a list of various statistics. It should generally conclude on the effectiveness of the firm's money laundering and terrorist financing deterrence systems and make recommendations for improvements.

Another benefit of producing such a report is that it is a helpful tool which enables the MLRO to document key money laundering and terrorist financing deterrence policies and procedures, identifying key issues of relevance to senior management.

Recommendations made by the MLRO in the report should then be considered by the firm's senior management. It is the role of the senior management to assess whether internal reports are being made when required and to consider whether figures revealed in the report could in fact conceal inadequate reporting. Having considered the report senior management will then need to take any necessary action to remedy any deficiencies identified by the report.

Annual reports made by the MLRO may cover all or any of the following information:

Nominated officer (or MLRO)

The name of the nominated officer should be stated, together with a summary report on their activities.

Director/senior management

The report should outline the demarcation of responsibilities between the MLRO and senior management of the firm, providing additional clarity as to the protections that are provided to the MLRO by relevant legislation.

MLRO functions

The responsibilities of the MLRO should be confirmed as well as highlighting any areas where the MLRO considers that they are restricted from carrying out their function. The report may also consider whether the MLRO has sufficient resources and access to information.

Staff training

The report should include information concerning the training of staff, including who has been trained, methods of training and any difficulties faced in achieving a satisfactory level of training. Any recommendations or improvements to training should also be considered.

Information to senior management

A description of the reporting procedure to senior management who receive reports should be included. The extent to which customer or counterparty names should be included in such reporting should also be considered since adding additional disclosure could potentially increase the risk of tipping off.

Documentation of policies and risk assessments

The report should describe arrangements for documentation of policies and risk assessments. The report may specifically describe how the firm uses local regulatory and statutory guidance. The report will typically identify deficiencies in current policies and reporting procedures, as well as outlining the seriousness of the issue and any recommendations for change. This part of the report may also comment on any new regulatory or legislative changes which will impact on the firm's risk management processes.

New products

As new products are introduced it will be important for the MLRO to consider to what extent they may potentially be used by people engaged in money laundering and terrorist financing, such that appropriate policies and procedures can be adopted prior to the product launch. In the report the MLRO will refer to the new products that either have been or are planned to be launched, consider the susceptibility to money laundering and terrorist financing and document the actions proposed or taken to mitigate such susceptibility.

Financially excluded

Many jurisdictions have specific rules requiring financial institutions to avoid excluding any specific customer grouping from the business conducted by the firm. Such rules can potentially run contrary to the objectives of the MLRO. Accordingly in the annual report the MLRO should describe the arrangements for dealing with customers who are financially excluded and their impact on the money laundering and terrorist financing regime adopted.

Arrangements for monitoring effectiveness of systems and controls

Normally the report will set out how the MLRO is achieving all of their objectives, including the maintenance of effective systems and controls. In this respect the contents of the report typically refer to the following in summary:

- The nature of the systems and controls operated by the business.
- Recommendations for the firm's systems and controls to ensure that they cover areas of:
    - the system for producing information provided to relevant agencies and to senior management;
    - the adequacy of relevant risk management policies and risk profiles;
    - the processes adopted in respect of new products, take-on of new customers and changes in business profile;
    - conclusions regarding the nature of employee acceptance and recruitment processes and procedures.

Summary of business areas

In their report the MLRO will generally outline the business operations and activities of the firm, highlighting how susceptible these are to use by criminal elements and the implications these then have on the money laundering and terrorist financing controls that are applied.

Customers and customer due diligence processes

Clearly the adequacy of customer due diligence remains at the heart of the work that the MLRO requires the business to undertake and accordingly this is generally also included in their annual report. Key elements of such a report will generally include the following:

- Details of the firm's customer base, including information on size, area of business, country of origin, percentage increases/ decreases and anything unusual.
- Information on the firm's politically exposed person (PEP) policies and procedures.
- The firm's arrangements for sanctions compliance, including information on procedures, checks, who is verified and the type of transactions that are checked.
- Details of arrangements where identification and due diligence are not carried out directly by the firm.
- The procedures which are used for identification verification, including any exceptions which may exist.
- Details as to how high risk customers are dealt with.
- Information on how know your client (KYC) information is collected, together with information if relevant concerning the implementation and modelling of the risk-based approach.
- The firm's arrangements for monitoring transactions.
- Information summarising the firm's product range and the risk that this poses to the firm in terms of its susceptibility to being used by criminal elements.
- Normally there is also a discussion of the geographical areas of operation of the business and any additional risks that this then poses.

Overall assessment of systems and controls

While customer due diligence is a fundamental part of the deterrence policies, ongoing controls, policies and procedures are also of significant importance. It is incumbent upon the MLRO to ensure that senior management and the regulators have a full and comprehensive understanding of the nature of the control environment employed by the firm, together with the conclusions as to the adequacy of such procedures. Accordingly the report normally will address the following issues:

- The nature of the systems and controls in place and whether they are comprehensive and proportionate.
- Whether such systems and controls have been regularly reviewed, by whom, and the conclusions that have arisen.
- Whether there have been any control failures. Any such failures will generally be identified, as well as any rule breaches and remedial action taken.

Record keeping

MLRO and firm record-keeping requirements do vary between jurisdictions, with many regulators undertaking reviews into both the adequacy of such records and their compliance with the relevant rules and regulations. Accordingly in their report the MLRO will typically wish to refer to the following matters:

- The format and location of where records are kept, together with any changes that have been made to the way the information is recorded or stored.
- Whether there have been any failures in controlling the record-keeping procedures as well as any recommendations for change.

Suspicious transaction reporting

This is also a fundamental part of the role of the MLRO, accordingly reference to this will generally also be made in the annual report, without highlighting specific details of individual cases identified and whether they were, or were not, reported. Matters that will generally be referred to in the report will include:

- An outline of the methods used to identify suspicious transactions and any limitations to this process.
- Any improvements, enhancements or proposed systems changes which the MLRO feels are necessary.
- A summary of the number of internal reports made by each business area.
- The number of internal reports which were not forwarded to the relevant money laundering authority. The report will also generally highlight whether this number has increased or decreased from previous years.

- Any circumstances which may have led to changes in reporting, and identify any possible trends.
- Any quality checks on reporting that are made by the MLRO.

External reporting

A separate section of the annual report normally provides the senior management and regulators with information regarding reporting actually made by the MLRO. The contents of this section will typically include the following matters:

- Whether there were any cases of money laundering where a report was not made.
- An analysis of the number of reports which were passed to money laundering authorities per business area.
- Any changes/trends in reporting.
- Any feedback from the relevant money laundering authority on reporting, whether individually or by sector.
- A review of any actions taken concerning noncooperative jurisdictions including any measures implemented within the firm.

Recommendations for action

This section should detail recommendations made by the MLRO to senior management. This should be described in order of priority areas of remedial and preventative action, as well as an expected time frame for action. The MLRO should also comment on the adequacy of resources as well as any recommendations for change.

Chapter 10

MONEY LAUNDERING TRAINING

THE IMPORTANCE OF STAFF AWARENESS AND TRAINING

Knowledge by staff of the key regulatory requirements that exist within their jurisdiction, together with what constitutes money laundering and terrorist financing, is absolutely critical. Accordingly maintaining adequate staff awareness and appropriate relevant training is an important element in any bank achieving its overall objective of combating money laundering and terrorist financing.

For any firm, to just have a series of rules, regulations, checks and balances would have limited effect if the employees who must implement the measures are inadequately trained and therefore unaware of these obligations. One of the most important controls over the prevention and detection of money laundering is to have staff that are alert to the risks of money laundering and terrorist financing, and that are well trained in the identification of unusual or suspicious activities.

It is essential that firms implement a complete and structured policy of training all relevant employees so that they are both aware of their personal obligations with regard to money laundering deterrence, whilst also understanding the role that they play in the overall achievement of appropriate money laundering deterrence within a financial institution. This will be of particular importance to staff that are customer facing and/or who handle customer transactions and instructions. Generally it is also sensible for such training to be extended to include temporary and contract staff carrying out similar customer facing functions. Clearly if training is appropriate for a full-time employee, then a contractor that undertakes the same role should be trained to a similar standard.

THE CORE OBLIGATIONS OF TRAINING

The core obligations of training staff with regard to money laundering deterrence and terrorist financing is so that relevant employees are:

- aware of the risks posed by money laundering and terrorist financing, the relevant legislation and their obligations under that legislation;

- made aware of the identity and responsibilities of the firm's nominated officer and money laundering reporting officer (MLRO);
- trained in the firm's procedures and in how to deal with potential money laundering or terrorist financing transactions or activity;
- made aware of how money laundering crimes operate and how they might take place through the firm;
- made aware of what actually might represent terrorist financing and how this would appear within their records;
- understand the legal position of the firm and of individual members of staff and of how these legal positions might change based upon the actions actually taken;
- understand how to operate a risk-based approach to anti-money laundering and terrorist financing.

LEGAL AND REGULATORY OBLIGATIONS

In many jurisdictions, including the United Kingdom, individual members of staff may face criminal penalties if they are involved in money laundering or terrorist financing, or if they fail to report their knowledge or suspicions when there are reasonable grounds to know or suspect money laundering activity. It is important that staff are made aware of these obligations, and that they are provided with sufficient training in how to discharge these obligations.

Regulators in most countries will detail what they require in respect of money laundering awareness and training. In the United Kingdom, the Financial Services Authority has published detailed rules which may be found in the FSA's sourcebook at: http://fsahandbook.info/FSA/html/handbook/TC. The main obligation placed by the FSA rules on senior management is that they must take measures to ensure that employees are made aware of laws which relate to money laundering and terrorist financing, and given training on how to deal with transactions related to money laundering.

The FSA suggests that a firm, when considering training and competence, ensures that:

- its employees achieve the right level of competence;
- its employees remain competent for the work they do;
- its employees are appropriately supervised;

- its employees' competence is regularly reviewed;
- the level of competence is appropriate to the nature of the business;
- an MLRO has been appointed with responsibility for oversight of the firm's anti-money laundering systems and controls, including appropriate training for employees (see Chapter 9).

Whilst these are the UK requirements, they would appear to be appropriate for all institutions globally.

In most countries failure by a firm to provide adequate training can result in severe consequences. Typically in the event that an employee fails to make a disclosure to its relevant agency when there were reasonable grounds for knowing or suspecting money laundering or terrorist financing, then there will be a liability on the employee and the firm. The penalties can be significant and include fines, restriction of activity, retraining or, at worst, prison.

If the employee that failed to make the report had not been provided with relevant and appropriate training suitable for their role, this will act as a defence for the employee involved, and an additional liability would then be imposed on the firm. A successful defence by the employee will leave the firm open to prosecution or regulatory sanction for failing to have adequate training and awareness training. Consequently the burden is on firms not only to obtain acknowledgement of training from individual employees, but also to take steps to ensure its effectiveness.

STAFF RESPONSIBILITIES

In order to comply with the overall obligations under the various money laundering legislation and regulations, responsibilities are distributed amongst the various employment levels within the firm.

Senior management

As we have discussed it is the responsibility of senior management to ensure that they have in place appropriate systems to combat money laundering and terrorist financing and therefore they need to have sufficient monitoring and reporting to enable them to actually know that these obligations are being met.

The maintenance of effective training arrangements is also the responsibility of the relevant director or senior manager. However it is normally the responsibility of the MLRO to ensure that the firm's compliance with money laundering measures are appropriate. This is normally achieved through their providing oversight in respect of training including taking reasonable steps to ensure the firm's systems and controls include appropriate training for employees. Remember that the requirements for training are normally for all staff and therefore should also extend to awareness training for senior management, MLROs and nominated officers.

The key training responsibility of the MLRO, including training for senior management, can be summarised as providing the guidance necessary to ensure that relevant employees are aware of:

- their responsibilities under the firm's arrangements for the prevention of money laundering and terrorist financing, including those for obtaining sufficient evidence of identity, recognising and reporting knowledge or suspicion of money laundering or terrorist financing;
- the identity and responsibilities for the nominated officer and the MLRO;
- the potential effect on the firm, on its employees personally and on its clients of any breach of that law.

Staff

As discussed above, it is the responsibility of senior management to ensure that all staff are aware of their personal responsibilities regarding anti-money laundering procedures at the start of their employment. These responsibilities should be clearly documented for ease of reference for the duration of their employment. Some of the unusual patterns of behaviour, transactions and scenarios that staff are advised to specifically look out for are detailed in Chapter 18.

Failure to report suspicions, tipping off those suspected of money laundering and prejudicing an investigation into money laundering or terrorist financing are all generally offences under relevant local legislation. In many cases the individual employee who tips off the client can be personally subject to some form of enforcement action. These offences would have an obvious application to those staff that engage in customer facing activity, but would also apply to back office staff. Accordingly it is important that all employees are provided with sufficient training, whether in the regulated sector or not.

INTERNAL TRAINING PROCEDURES

The rules therefore require that specialised training must be provided to all of a firm's employees. This training should explain to employees how the products and services offered by the firm may be used as a vehicle for money laundering or terrorist financing. This is because unless the training appears to be applicable to the nature of the business being conducted, there will be little obvious relevance to the day-to-day work of the employees.

The training should also explain the firm's procedures and the methods it uses to manage these risks. The legal liabilities both to the firm and to its employees will need to be explained to highlight how important this training actually is. Employees should be informed how the firm itself may be at risk of prosecution if suspicious transactions are proceeded with in the absence of consent from the relevant authorities. As a starting point, employees should be informed of what they need to know in terms of their particular role and what they should do if they become suspicious regarding either a case of money laundering or terrorist financing. Depending on the level of interaction that employees have with customers and customer data, the different roles will require different training tailored to their particular function. Customers may need to be informed of know your customer requirements as well as the importance of customer identification procedures and how to monitor customer activity.

Relevant employees should also be made aware of particular circumstances or customers who present a higher risk of money laundering or terrorist financing, or who are financially excluded. Training should therefore include information on the additional work to confirm identity that should be undertaken in such cases, and any additional local steps or reporting that should be made.

Staff must also be made aware of the changing behaviour and practices amongst money launderers and those financing terrorism. FATF's Guidance for Financial Institutions in Detecting Terrorist Financing contains an in-depth analysis of the methods used in the financing of terrorism and the types of financial activities constituting potential indicators of such activities. These documents, which are continuously updated, are available at www.fatf-gafi.org. In the UK information concerning risk profiles and threat assessments is published by the Serious Organised Crime Agency which can be found at www.soca.gov.uk. Furthermore in the UK, illustrations of real case studies of how individuals and organisations might raise funds and how financial products may be used by money launderers are published by the Joint Money Laundering Steering Group and can be found at www.jmlsg.org.uk. All of this material is suitable for inclusion in training materials.

TRAINING METHODS AND ASSESSMENT

There are various ways in which firms may decide to carry out staff training, and the approach adopted will of course depend on the method that best suits the firm whilst achieving the objectives of local regulations. The approach that would be adopted by a firm that has all of their employees at one site will be different to the approach that would be suitable for a firm which has staff distributed over a range of sites.

Employees who work with high risk customers or in more specialist areas of finance may require more direct and tailored classroom-based learning than would be suitable for the generality of staff. Distributing training videos within a firm may stimulate interest, but continually showing the same video may produce diminishing returns. Further it becomes extremely difficult to know the level of attention that has been given by a specific employee to such training without some form of assessment procedure being conducted in addition to viewing the video.

As an alternative to such generic materials, specific training highlighting issues inherent within a firm's procedure manuals are useful in raising staff awareness and supplementing other forms of training. The main benefits of such a form of training are that they are tailored to the specific needs of a group of employees and will appear immediately relevant to the work being conducted on a day-to-day basis.

It is recommended that all training is ongoing and given at appropriate intervals to all relevant employees. Particularly in larger firms, this may take the form of a rolling programme. Once a method of training has been chosen, it is vital to establish comprehensive records in order to monitor who has been trained, when the training was received and the nature and effectiveness of training provided. As previously mentioned, this is also carried out by a firm to provide evidence of its compliance with AML legislation, as well as in the event that a firm is held liable when an employee's actions are called into question. Accordingly the assessment process and its recording are also of paramount importance.

Providing an email update to staff, or allowing them to view a film in their own time, is unlikely to be adequate without some formal process of assessment. Typically a short examination based on multiple choice questions will be suitable – with perhaps 10 questions being the typical length of an assessment. If a delegate fails twice on a multiple choice question then you would expect that they would have to view the training materials again before resitting the examination.

Chapter 11

KNOW YOUR CUSTOMER

WHAT IS KNOW YOUR CUSTOMER?

The basic and most essential feature of all anti-money laundering legislation and regulations all over the world is the need for appropriate and adequate customer due diligence. Such due diligence is to enable the bank to really understand the customer and the risks they pose both to the firm and to society at large. The level and depth of the analysis will need to be commensurate with the risks that the relationship poses. Clearly it will not be sufficient for the firm to just accept information which is provided to them by customers at face value. Some level of investigation should be undertaken to establish that the documents are indeed valid and that they may be used to confirm and support customer information and identification. Failure to do so could result in obviously fraudulent documents being accepted in error, with potentially serious consequences.

Regulations that are implemented within individual jurisdictions are likely to specify individual due diligence requirements that should be conducted. These could either represent a general requirement imposed on the firm that they should understand their clients; or more detailed rules and regulations specifying the precise work to be conducted in specific situations as know your customer (KYC) requirements.

KYC is essentially the work conducted by a firm to undertake background checks on clients and customers to enable them to both obtain and confirm additional information regarding their customers. Detailed enquiries should be able to validate documents and information provided by the customer, together with substantiating claims regarding the source of funds. However in many cases firms purely record the source of funds on the KYC rather than actually proving that the source is appropriate. In the next two chapters we consider specific requirements with regard to both retail and corporate customers.

Increasingly it is being viewed by regulatory authorities in sophisticated financial centres that it is not enough merely to know your customer through identification documents. They expect that the firm's investigations would critically examine the information provided to test its validity. Such checks will typically occur at the beginning of any financial relationship where the accepting business must satisfy itself that the new customer that enters into a financial transaction or business relationship is an appropriate customer to do business with.

This work is closely linked to both customer relationship management and the selling process. Firms need to undertake adequate work to confirm that the product being sold to the customer is appropriate to their needs and requirements. As such every sale made by a firm should include some element of KYC completion. This information can also be used by a firm to identify products that would typically be purchased by customers with this specific profile, leading to additional income for the firm.

Therefore there are many reasons for a firm to maintain KYC information and the requirements are therefore standard procedural requirements. Since the requirement is not just dependent on the regulations relating to money laundering and the financing of terrorism, firms are able to use selling compliance rules and customer relationship management requirements to enable them to obtain the information that they may also require to meet money laundering deterrence and terrorist financing obligations.

As part of the battle against money laundering and terrorist financing, the importance of a firm carrying out adequate KYC due diligence procedures can never be underestimated. Inadequate KYC due diligence may make the difference between a transaction being carried out and not being carried out; and a firm being prosecuted or not prosecuted. If an entity cannot obtain sufficient details to adequately establish the customer's identity or if there are any suspicions about the background of the customer, customer relations should generally not be established. However the customer should not be notified that the relationship has not been proceeded with due to money laundering concerns, since this would represent tipping off (see Chapter 20).

WHY SHOULD FIRMS CARRY OUT KYC REQUIREMENTS?

Generally the due diligence carried out by a firm on new customers is in two distinct parts. As well as verifying their identity, the risk-based approach will lead to a need, in appropriate cases, to obtain additional information in respect of some customers. Clear policies and procedures are required to ensure that such requirements are rigorously complied with in all cases where such enhanced due diligence procedures are required. These KYC checks are designed to:

1. understand the customer's circumstances and business – including, where appropriate, the source of funds, and in some cases the source of wealth;
2. understand the purpose of specific transactions;
3. understand the expected nature and level of transactions; and ensure that information maintained is both current and valid.

The firm should consider the risk of a relationship being related to money laundering based on their client portfolio and their range of services in determining the extent and nature of due diligence to be conducted. A standard approach should be adopted to the identification of customers using a series of appropriate checklists, with additional information being required where the risk profile of a particular client or class of client and/or service requires it.

WHAT DOES KYC INVOLVE?

Usually this system of control involves taking identification in some prescribed form. Typically documents such as National Identity Cards, passports and driving licences are recommended to be taken and the details contained on them recorded, and kept for a designated number of years. Records are usually kept for up to five years from the date of the transaction (for a one-off transaction) and for a period after the end of the relationship with the client in the case of longer and multiple transactions.

Specific requirements in respect of retail customers are addressed in Chapter 12, and in respect of corporate customers in Chapter 13.

WHAT ARE THE GENERAL ISSUES?

Reluctance to provide information

Banks will find that in practice there is a pattern to the type of things that can go wrong, which need to be included in awareness training for staff. Some of these are included within this section. One example is any cases where new business or personal customers are reluctant to provide information on their normal activities, location and directors. It must be emphasised that this does not mean the customer is money laundering; they may simply have inappropriate concerns about sharing their personal information.

However there have been cases of actual money laundering which would have been recognised had the suspicion identified initially on the opening of the account been thoroughly investigated.

Conflicting information

Another concern is new personal customers that supply incomplete, conflicting or incongruous information when establishing a relationship. Many customers will initially provide incomplete information; indeed you have probably done so yourself. This alone would not be reason for enhanced due diligence to be conducted. However if there are repeated problems, or information is regularly corrected, then this would raise additional awareness of the risks of inappropriate conduct occurring.

Provision of key data

Customers that do not provide addresses, phone or fax numbers, or those for whom the numbers provided relate to serviced office/ accommodation addresses, are also high risk. The problem here is that the customer is not enabling the firm to make regular contact with them and may only be temporarily where they are currently working. A firm can easily set up what appears to be an office in a serviced office suite, then leave the following day.

Firms should always check phone numbers and addresses, visiting where appropriate and reviewing phone listings which are publicly available. In many cases firms will undertake credit reference agency searches to ensure that the customer has provided what appear to be consistent data sets.

Fraudulent information

Firms need to be aware of the risks associated with identification documents, for example the problems caused by camouflage passports. A camouflage passport is a passport issued in the name of a nonexistent country that is intended to look like a real country's passport. Such passports are also often sold with several matching documents, including an international driver's licence and similar supporting identity papers.

Camouflage passports are generally issued in names of countries that no longer exist or have changed their name, for example Burma or Ceylon. Others use the names of places or political subdivisions that exist within a real country, but that have never issued and cannot issue passports, for example Zurich or New York. Still others are issued in the names of wholly fictitious countries that typically have a plausible name or one that is close to the name of a real country, for example Koristan (which is a place in Turkey) or the Simon Islands (there is a St Simon's Island in the Caribbean).

It is important for the original passport to be seen – a photocopy is generally not enough. The firm may accept a copy of a passport which has been authorised by a notary public and will always keep a copy of the passport on file. The date and time when the passport was received should ideally also be recorded to highlight that such procedures were undertaken prior to transactions actually being carried out.

Diplomatic passports

Another concern is diplomats generally and in particular diplomatic passports from relatively small or new countries. Such passports may be genuine (i.e., genuinely issued after payment), however this does not mean that the holder is genuine or the name shown on the passport is the real one. The firm may not even have an awareness of what a passport from that country actually looks like.

Source: http://upload.wikimedia.org/wikipedia/commons/thumb/4/4d/Inside_of_an_azerbaijani_passport.JPG/200px

In other countries there can be multiple types of passport available, as shown in the next image:

Source: http://upload.wikimedia.org/wikipedia/commons/thumb/9/9f/LV-pase-3.jpg/300px-LV-pase-3.jpg

Always the firm should attempt to evaluate whether the other details given, together with the appearance and attitude of the customer, appear to be consistent with the information being provided. In the case of a diplomat the person's persona should match whatever diplomatic post he/she is claiming to hold.

In a 2007 case Vladimir Kuznetsov, a former Russian diplomat to the United Nations, was convicted of money laundering in the US courts and returned to Russia to serve his sentence. His crime was to launder in excess of $300 000 which, it had been alleged, related to companies seeking contracts to supply the United Nations with goods and services. Mr Kuznetsov was Russia's highest serving UN diplomat and served as Chairman of the UN Advisory Committee on Administrative and Budgetary Questions. A former colleague who served as a procurement officer at the UN testified against Kuznetsov and pleaded guilty in 2005 to having committed both wire fraud and money laundering, accepting in excess of $1m generated by the scheme. The financial penalty on Kuznetsov of only $73 671 appeared rather low although it was supported by 4 years 3 months of a prison term.

Financial information

In the course of receiving corporate due diligence materials the firm will receive financial information regarding the nature of the business to be conducted. As will be discussed further in Chapter 13, firms should review such material to identify whether the level of activity appears consistent with the size and scope of the firm's activities.

Too fast

Another area of suspicion is the rushing customer. If a group of accounts or relationships are opened by foreign nationals who visit your organisation together on the same day, then this is potentially a process designed to put your due diligence procedures under pressure. There should be enhanced due diligence in such cases even if this does mean there will be a delay in opening the account. A situation that is far more difficult to identify is where multiple accounts or relationships are opened on the same day by a group of foreign nationals at different banks/companies in the same city.

Similar suspicions should be aroused if multiple business relationships are opened by an individual using the same address, or different individuals using the same address. Additionally definite suspicion should result if numerous accounts or relationships are established using variations of the same name, for example Risky Reward Limited, Reward Risk Limited and Riskreward Limited.

RELIANCE ON THIRD PARTIES

Historically firms used to rely heavily on work conducted by other banks and also work conducted by their branches and subsidiaries. This is no longer considered appropriate and penalties have arisen where firms have relied for identification solely on this basis. Generally each office should conduct its own due diligence since without undertaking such analysis it will be difficult for them to have sufficient understanding of the nature of the customer for them to identify unusual transactions warranting investigation.

If there is a branch/head office relationship it may be appropriate for the relevant work to be conducted once but provided to both offices. In all cases the rules of the local jurisdiction should be reviewed and complied with in this respect.

THE THIRD EC DIRECTIVE – KYC REQUIREMENTS

The Third EC Directive provides consolidated guidance on anti-money laundering procedures to Member States of the European Community. As always with EC legislation, Member States are under an obligation to adopt these rules and implement them into their national laws and legislation. Article 8 of the Third EC Directive outlines the following basic KYC procedures:

(a) Identifying the customer and verifying the customer's identification should be undertaken on the basis of documents. Data or information should be obtained from a reliable and independent source.
(b) Financial institutions should identify, where applicable, the beneficial owner of an account. They should undertake risk-based adequate measures to verify their identity so that the institution or person covered by this Directive is satisfied that it knows who the beneficial owner is, including as regards legal persons, trusts and similar legal arrangements, taking risk-based and adequate measures to understand the ownership and control structure of the customer.
(c) They should obtain information regarding the purpose and intended nature of the business relationship.
(d) They should conduct ongoing monitoring of the business relationship including scrutiny of transactions undertaken throughout the course of that relationship to ensure that the transactions being conducted are consistent with the institution's or person's knowledge of the customer, the business and risk profile including, where necessary, the source of funds and to ensure that documents, data or information held are kept up-to-date.

Additional enhanced due diligence requirements exist for particular circumstances which relate to:

- beneficial owners not clearly identified
- dealing with non face-to-face customers
- international correspondent banking
- politically exposed persons
- anonymous accounts
- casinos.

Generally there is a requirement that Member States must ensure that institutions and persons covered under the Directive apply due diligence measures to existing and new customers on a risk-sensitive basis.

THE UK KYC REQUIREMENTS

The Joint Money Laundering Steering Group (JMLSG) Prevention of Money Laundering/Combating Terrorist Financing Rules, consolidates all UK AML legislation including the Money Laundering Regulations 2007 to provide industry guidance to the UK financial sector. This is discussed in Chapter 4. The KYC requirements are referred to in the Guidance as CDD (Customer Due Diligence) measures, and are essentially the same concept. The KYC/CDD requirements contained in this Guidance aim to consolidate previous KYC requirements.

Required CDD

The Guidance aims to help a firm to determine the extent of CDD measures which they must undertake. CDD measures which a firm wishes to carry out must be determined on a risk-sensitive basis, taking into account the type of customer, business relationship, product or transaction. Firms must be able to demonstrate that their CDD procedures are appropriate in view of the risks of money laundering and terrorist financing.

CDD measures must be carried out by firms when they:

- establish a business relationship;
- carry out an occasional transaction;
- suspect money laundering or terrorist funding;
- doubt the veracity of documents, data or information previously obtained for the purpose of identification or verification.

CDD procedures that must be conducted include:

- **Identifying the customer and verifying their identity** The firm identifies the customer by obtaining a range of information about them. The verification of the identity consists of the firm verifying some of this information against documents, data or information obtained from a reliable independent source.

- **Identifying the beneficial owner, where relevant, and verifying their identity** A beneficial owner is normally an individual who ultimately owns or controls the customer or on whose behalf a transaction or activity is being conducted. In respect of private individuals the customer himself is the beneficial owner, unless there are features of the transaction or surrounding circumstances that indicate otherwise. Therefore, there is no requirement on firms to make proactive searches for beneficial owners in such cases, but they should make appropriate enquiries where it appears that the customer is not acting on his own behalf.

Where an individual is required to be identified as a beneficial owner, where a customer who is a private individual is fronting for another individual who is the beneficial owner, the firm should obtain the same information about that beneficial owner as it would for a customer. The identity of a customer must be verified on the basis of documents, data or information obtained from a reliable independent source. The obligation to verify the identity of a beneficial owner is for the firm to take risk-based and adequate measures so that it is satisfied that it knows who the beneficial owner is. It is up to each firm whether they make use of records of beneficial owners in the public domain (if any exist), ask their customers for relevant data or obtain the information otherwise. There is no specific requirement to have regard to particular types of evidence.

In lower risk situations therefore it may be reasonable for firms to be satisfied as to the beneficial owner's identity based on information supplied by the customer. This includes information provided by the customer (including trustees or other representatives whose identities have been verified) as to their identity, and confirmation that they are known to the customer. While this may be provided orally or in writing, any information received orally should be recorded in written form by the firm.

- **Obtaining information on the purpose and intended nature of the business relationship** A firm must understand the purpose and indeed the nature of the business relationship or transaction. In some instances this will be self-evident, but in many cases the firm may have to obtain information in this regard. Depending on the firm's risk assessment of the situation, information that might be relevant includes some or all of the following:
    - the nature and details of the business/occupation/ employment;
    - the record of changes of address;
    - the expected source and origin of the funds to be used in the relationship;
    - initial and ongoing sources of wealth income (particularly within a private banking or wealth management relationship);
    - copies of recent and current financial statements;

- ○ the various relationships between signatories and with underlying beneficial owners;
- ○ the anticipated level and nature of the activity that is to be undertaken through the relationship.

Quality and quantity of CDD

Evidence of identity can take a number of forms. In the UK rules in respect of individuals much weight is placed on so-called "identity documents", such as passports and photo card driving licences, and these are often the easiest way of being reasonably satisfied as to someone's identity. It is also possible to be reasonably satisfied of a customer's identity based on other forms of confirmation, including written assurances from persons or organisations that have dealt with the customer for some time.

How much information to ask for and what to verify, in order to be reasonably satisfied as to a customer's identity, are matters of judgement of the firm. These must be exercised on a risk-based approach, taking into account the following factors:

- the nature of the product or service sought by the customer (any other products or services to which they can migrate without further identity verification);
- the nature and length of any existing or previous relationship with the customer and the firm;
- the nature and extent of assurances from other regulated firms that may be relied on;
- whether the customer is physically present.

Documentary evidence used as part of KYC

Documentation purporting to offer evidence of identity may emanate from a number of sources, with differing levels of reliability and integrity. The broad hierarchy of documents include:

- certain documents issued by government departments and agencies or by a court;
- certain documents issued by other public bodies or local authorities;
- certain documents issued by regulated firms in the financial services sector;

- certain documents issued by those subject to ML Regulations or equivalent legislation;
- documents issued by other organisations.

Firms should recognise the fact that some documents are more easily forged than others. If suspicions are raised in relation to any document offered, firms should take practical and proportionate steps to establish whether the document has been lost or stolen. Thus firms must also have in place procedures, and be prepared to accept a range of documents. They may also wish to employ electronic checks, either on their own or in tandem with documentary evidence.

Chapter 12

RETAIL CUSTOMER IDENTIFICATION

WHO ARE RETAIL CUSTOMERS?

Retail customers are essentially private individuals who act in their own capacity. Customer identification procedures that are suitable for personal customers will inevitably be different from those that are applied to corporate customers. This is due to the nature of the relationship and also the nature of the documentation that is available to the financial institution.

Of course in corporate relationships it may still be appropriate to identify some of the owners, controllers or stakeholders depending on the nature of the relationship. In such cases the process that is undertaken is similar to that addressed in this chapter and will be in addition to the procedures discussed in Chapter 13 concerning corporate customers.

While this might, on first consideration, appear to be a straightforward distinction, the line between retail customers and corporate customers is not always clear cut. Consider the case of an individual that forms themselves into a company. Should the corporate rules be applied for identification, or the retail rules? What if the customer has one assistant? Would that make such a difference?

In practice you will find that firms do operate different approaches. What is important is that, regardless of the approach adopted, sufficient information is obtained to enable the firm to really understand the nature of the customer's activity. The firm should have a clear policy which sets out the requirements in all such cases with the objective always being to obtain sufficient reliable evidence to provide the firm with the protection it requires demonstrating that appropriate procedures have been complied with. In making such an assessment the firm should consider the nature of the risk that the relationship introduces and conduct such analysis as appears appropriate in the circumstances.

BASIC RETAIL IDENTIFICATION EVIDENCE

Firms must generally initially identify private individuals by obtaining three key pieces of information;

- the full name;
- residential address; and
- date of birth.

However this information must be obtained from reliable and independent sources. It is not sensible just to ask the customer to provide the data to the firm since that will not provide any evidence of independent review. Instead reference should be made to reliable documents that are prepared by a third party (agency or government, for example). In particular, photocopies should not be accepted unless they have clearly been authorised by an appropriate legal resource.

Typical documents required include the passport, driving licence or identity card, together with some form of utility or other bill that will prove the address. The key element is having at least one piece of evidence that includes the face of the customer so that it can be confirmed by the financial institution by actually meeting the person. Of course any of these documents could be forged – a utility bill is quite capable of being forged on a photocopier.

In terms of specific requirements, reference will need to be made to local rules since these do vary. Clearly firms should take particular care when dealing with customers that they do not meet face-to-face. The objective is always where possible to see originals of documents when verifying identity, but non face-to-face customers are likely to be reluctant to send valuable original documentation through the post. This leads to the problems of dealing with non face-to-face customers as discussed in Chapter 15.

DOCUMENTARY VERIFICATION

Once retail customer documents have been produced by the customer on request, the firm is still under an obligation to conduct validation procedures to ensure that they are reliable. The highest quality documentation which firms can place reliance on will be documentary evidence issued by a government department or agency. The logic for this is that government agencies can in theory be relied upon to have undertaken procedures to verify their own evidence, checking the existence and characteristics of the person concerned.

The evidence obtained must give the firm reasonable confidence in the customer's identity which the firm should weigh against the risks involved in relying on this evidence. Non government-issued documentary evidence may be accepted if it originated from a public sector body or a firm regulated by the financial services and in other cases this may be used to provide supporting evidence.

Government-issued documents which incorporate a full name, address, date of birth and photograph, typically include the following:

- valid passport;
- valid driving licence including a photograph of the customer;
- national identity card, ideally also including a photograph of the customer.

There may be other documents acceptable to a firm for identification specified by the regulations, but these are normally only acceptable when two pieces of identification documentation are required, which is the position in some countries.

One of the concerns is forgery. A passport which has almost no stamps in it with a photograph that looks exactly like the customer is likely to be a higher risk of forgery than a passport that looks like the customer on a bad day with a load of individual country stamps. The forger will not generally also forge country stamps.

Government-issued documents without a photograph may also be used for customer identification, as long as they incorporate the customer's full name and are supported by a second document which is government-issued, or issued by a judicial or public sector authority or a regulated firm which incorporates full name, address and date of birth. In the UK utility companies can also meet this requirement, but we would recommend caution. Any piece of evidence that can be forged on a photocopier must by its very nature be considered as limited evidence. Such documents are normally only used to verify address data, although this may be independently available in some form of electoral roll documentation – or even the telephone book.

Generally speaking, face-to-face verification can be achieved by the customer producing a valid passport or photocard licence and the firm confirming that the picture shown is a reasonable likeness of the customer. Remember that if the picture is a perfect likeness then this may also provide cause for concern since the money launderer always has perfect documents.

Generally the provision of such documents should enable individuals to meet identification requirement for money laundering deterrence purposes. However, they may not be sufficient in themselves, and consequently firms will need to apply a risk-based approach when determining the level of additional identification checks to be conducted – generally referred to as enhanced due diligence. Firms may wish to pay particular attention to managing fraud or credit risk, and so may restrict the use of certain identification documents. This will depend on the current status of forgery in their country. Indeed it is the reducing cost of forged documents which is such a concern at present.

In the UK the obligations have moved towards really understanding your customer and away from simple narrow requirements, which is clearly appropriate. It does of course raise additional problems for banks that are not dealing directly with their customers in person, for example internet banks and credit card vendors. Accordingly a higher level of additional verification is required in such cases.

CUSTOMER EXCLUSION

In most countries there are specific rules on financial exclusion and this can lead to some unusual cases. How would you identify the street vendor who does not have a permanent address and is perhaps illiterate? In practice firms may be willing to accept a symbol made by the customer who is unable to sign their name and will also undertake and record additional procedures.

If you have rules requiring a passport or driving licence and another form of identity then there will be some customers that will not have such documents. If you consider the case of a teenage child they may have a passport, but no other documentation. Clearly a letter of reference from the parent should be acceptable as additional identification, but this historically was not allowed in the UK. In one case a teenage customer of a bank, whom I shall refer to as Robert, wanted to open another account at the same bank. He had a passport, but since he lived with his parents did not have either a utility bill or a driving licence. The bank rejected their own documents as evidence and told Robert to take £1 to another bank up the road.

Using the first bank's bank statement and the passport he would be able to open an account at the second bank. With the information from the second bank he could return to the first bank and use this additional information to open an account. This is regulation that is clearly ineffective and has fortunately, in the case of the UK, been repealed.

ELECTRONIC VERIFICATION

Electronic verification of identity should be carried out by a firm using the customer's name, address and date of birth to carry out an electronic check directly or through a supplier (for example a commercial agency such as Experian). Electronic verification provides additional independent assurance that the customer is who they say they are. Even electronic verification needs to meet a standard level of confirmation before it can be relied upon by a financial institution. To be acceptable there needs to be a match for the individual's name or current address, and a second match on an individual's name, with their current address or date of birth. When firms use commercial agencies for electronic verification they must ensure that they fully understand the systems and scoring mechanisms used by the firm when interpreting the results. There should always be a manual review of any such documents in case of manifest error by the agency.

Firms should remember that although outsourcing of a role to a commercial agency is permitted, they can delegate the work but not abrogate responsibility. Accordingly a measure of supervision would need to still be maintained. There is a specific Bank for International Settlements paper which deals with outsourcing to which reference should be made for specific guidance to be adopted in such cases, including the documentation to be maintained and the maintenance of suitable service level agreements (SLAs) which must be effectively monitored.

IMPERSONATION FRAUD

Impersonation fraud (or phishing) has become an increasing problem in recent years and is probably the fastest growing area of fraud in the modern world. There are many reasons why a firm should manage the risk of impersonation fraud, only one of which relates to money laundering deterrence. The greatest risk is of course fraud and the disappearance of the customer with the funds of the firm, together with the reputational impact when this is discovered. There are greater risks in this respect when a firm is using electronic data to carry out additional anti-fraud checks as part of its routine procedures. In such cases the firm should implement additional due diligence procedures which incorporate the following:

- Requiring the first payment to be carried out in an account in the customer's name with a locally regulated credit institution, or one from an equivalent jurisdiction.
- Verifying additional aspects of a customer's identity using independent third party sources.
- Making telephone contact with the customer prior to opening the account on a home or business number which has been verified electronically, or making what is referred to as a "welcome call" to the customer before transactions are permitted. This is used to verify additional aspects of personal identity information that have previously been provided by the customer during the process leading to the set-up of the account.
- Communicating with the customer at an address that has been independently verified, e.g., direct mailing. Firms should not rely solely on addresses provided by the customer since this would increase the risk of fraud.
- Other card or account activation procedures, all of which should be clearly documented and understood by all staff. Firms need to make sure that all procedures are rigorously applied and that there is no ability for an employee to override the requirement to undertake a procedure. Such inappropriate activity would enable staff to assist in fraudulent activity being conducted.

FAMILY MEMBERS

There is generally no requirement to verify the identity of any other family members of the customer, or any requirement to obtain information on them. The rules tend to follow a simple legal view in that it is the customer that is opening the account, not the family. Accordingly information on family members is generally not recorded. In some countries it would be illegal to even make such enquiries.

Of course this does increase risk. If the spouse of the customer has been found guilty of money laundering, terrorist financing or fraud then this would clearly be relevant to a firm's assessment of the customer. That such enquiries cannot officially be made has the effect of increasing the opportunity for abuse of the system. Clearly if a firm does undertake any such review then it must not be documented if such documentation would breach local rules. There can always be another reason to reject a customer.

TRANSACTION MONITORING

In terms of accounts that are maintained with customers, the level of updating that is required to take place subsequent to the original account opening varies considerably between jurisdictions. In some countries if a retail customer had taken out a property loan they would need to provide details of their current employer such that a deduction could be made from their salary. Changes in employer likewise must immediately be reported.

In other cases all such loans are recorded on a central government database. The alternative is the situation in countries such as the UK where the customer is under no obligation whatsoever to provide up-to-date information to the firm. Accordingly the firm will not even know who the customer is employed by – only who they were employed by when they took out the facility. Clearly this severely impacts the ability of the firm to identify what might be considered as inappropriate transactions.

What a firm should do is to consider the nature of the information available to them and undertake such monitoring as they consider appropriate in the circumstances to provide them with the assurance that they believe they require. This is often in addition to the requirements of local regulations.

SOURCE OF FUNDS

Firms are generally required to record the source of funds for a deposit or repayment by a customer. However the rules rarely require this to be verified, which is perhaps rather unusual and renders the process pointless. If we take a case where a customer deposits $35 000, then they might say that the money was a gift from a friend, a legacy from a deceased relative or the proceeds from the sale of a car. The firm will record this, but they are not under any obligation to see if the customer actually had a friend, relative or car.

It is difficult to imagine that the money launderer will be caught out by this test. They are hardly likely to say that they were drug trafficking, for example. It is however an unusual pattern of behaviour which the firm should be able to identify and therefore detect inappropriate conduct.

Generally this is an area where the rules are really only requiring a process, rather than seeking to actually ensure that reliable evidence is obtained. The firm should still consider whether there is any evidence that might suggest that the funds may not be from the suggested source. The suspicion could result from the way that the funds are received, or from the illogicality of the information provided. If there are repeated legacies, for example, from the same parent, then this could be a cause for concern. You generally only die once.

Chapter 13

CORPORATE CUSTOMER IDENTIFICATION

WHO IS A CORPORATE CUSTOMER?

There are many different forms of corporate customer ranging from listed companies, through private limited liability companies to partnerships, trusts and charities. Corporate customers that are public companies listed on stock exchanges will already be subject to market regulation and higher levels of public disclosure, in terms of their ownership and business activities. Their accounts will be subject to external audit by an independent firm and their results will be analysed by the media. Such corporate customers may be considered as lower risk due to the level of scrutiny that clearly exists, although such firms could still be involved in inappropriate activity.

In the UK there are unlisted securities exchanges which appear to be listed but still have reasonably high levels of scrutiny. Larger unlisted companies will still be subject to higher levels of public disclosure and an external audit. It is this level of public exposure which makes corporate customers particularly concerned about money laundering risks. Such firms will no more wish to be involved with money laundering or terrorist financing than would be the case for the bank.

The key problem is that detailed information concerning such companies, such as company accounts, is easily accessible public information. Clearly companies can be particularly vulnerable to the criminal intentions of money launderers since they can access such information to use to their advantage. It is therefore advisable for firms, in their verification processes, to take into account that public information may be manipulated by money launderers to disguise their illegitimate objectives, stealing the identity of a legitimate business to cover their activity.

There are different problems in respect of family-owned and smaller companies. In such cases there is a limited level of independent verification and differing expectations on the role of the auditor. In the case of smaller corporates there might not even be a requirement for the firm to have external auditors, or for an audit to be conducted. The bank will need to consider this when taking documentation and consider whether additional procedures should be undertaken.

RISKS ASSOCIATED WITH CORPORATE CUSTOMERS

It may not always be particularly obvious why a corporate customer might in some cases pose a higher risk to money laundering than a private customer. Identification verification in the form of due diligence is important in the case of corporate customers for a number of reasons, not least of which are the local regulations promulgated within your jurisdiction.

There are things that, again, should suggest that a company is a higher risk than normal and therefore enhanced due diligence procedures should be conducted. One of these is the issue of businesses with particularly complex structures or ownership. In the case of the major fraud at Enron it was through taking advantage of accounting rules and operating complex structures that the losses of the firm were hidden for so long. In this case the audit could not be relied upon to identify the fraud – indeed it is important to remember that external auditors are not seeking to identify fraud in the design of their work.

The existence of a particularly complex business structure may mean that the financial institution must undertake additional measures to be reasonably satisfied of the identities of their business customers. The very existence of a complex structure will in itself also need to be investigated since this could be used to hide inappropriate activity, including potentially tax evasion. Again it is not just the money laundering concern that worries the firm; rather it is the losses that would occur were the company found to actually represent a fraud. Firms must be satisfied that there is an obvious legitimate commercial purpose for a corporate customer's business structure. If firms are unable to demonstrate such a legitimate purpose, then the financial institution should be alerted to the increased risk of potential money laundering or terrorist financing.

Another factor of concern when dealing with corporate customers is the extent of control given to individuals through a direct shareholding. Shareholders can exercise significant control over a company through their decision-making powers. They may have the power to make decisions regarding the management of funds and transactions without requiring specific additional authority. Thus, shareholders are in some cases able to override internal procedures and controls. A lack of internal control and regulations is typically the type of condition which a money launderer would exploit for his own illegitimate purposes.

However, a firm would not assume that, in all cases where shareholders exercise a significant level of control, they may be using the company's corporate structure to disguise money laundering activity. A high level of shareholder control is merely a situation which firms must investigate further on a risk-sensitive basis. Levels of control within corporate entities may depend on the nature of the company, the distribution of shareholdings, and the nature and extent of any business or family connections between the beneficial owners.

BENEFICIAL OWNERS

In order to conduct thorough due diligence on a corporate customer, firms will need to identify key individuals within the corporate structure. Typically such a figure is one that:

- ultimately owns or controls (whether through direct or indirect ownership or control, including through bearer shareholdings) more than 25% of the shares or voting rights in the body; or
- otherwise exercises control over the management of the body.

You will note that directors do not necessarily fall within this definition, unless the director is a beneficial owner or has a controlling influence. Directors are excluded if they do not have an ownership interest in the body, or do not control voting rights, or exercise control over management in the sense that enables them to manipulate voting and composition of the board of directors.

Of course a firm may still wish to identify signatories to the accounts of the customer, if only to make sure that they are passing some of the risk back to the customer. Signature verification will again need to have some form of document possibly produced by the legal function or company secretary. No additional work is normally undertaken in such cases.

STANDARD EVIDENCE FOR CORPORATE ENTITIES

Firms must start by asking corporate customers to produce evidence of the existence of the corporate structure that they are claiming to be. This will usually include:

- confirmation of the company's listing (if relevant);
- a search of the relevant companies registry;
- a copy of the company's Certificate of Incorporation;
- a copy of the documents forming the entity (for trusts, partnerships and similar structures);
- the memorandum and articles of association (even though these are both standard and easily available).

The standard identification evidence which all corporate customers must provide is generally as follows:

- full name;
- registered number;
- registered office in country of incorporation;
- business address.

Private and unlisted companies will usually also be required to provide:

- names of all directors (or equivalent);
- names of individuals who own or control over 25% of its shares or voting rights.

Notice we are stating that the information needs to be provided, not verified. While there is no specific requirement to obtain additional evidence to support the information provided by the corporate customer, we would always recommend that where possible a firm should obtain such information. Given the existence of the internet, trade journals and registration bodies, additional information to confirm data provided by the corporate customer is generally available. Again the telephone book may be a source of evidence, together with accounts filed at a central registry.

Just as for a personal customer, in the case of a corporate customer there is rarely a requirement to confirm the source of funds. The limit of such verification is normally checking a credit rating agency and the company registry in the country, together with obtaining the accounts. This work is not normally done with money laundering deterrence in mind, but for other reasons. In some countries there is a requirement to obtain the memorandum and articles of association of the company, but these are generally all standard documents.

The firm needs to undertake sufficient work to ensure that the company is the firm that it believes it is and to identify those persons that will be acting on the account. As such they will need to look at a variety of sources of information including information that is not obtained directly from the firm itself, but is obtained from third party agencies or public sources. If all of the information is received directly from the company then it is not independent and this clearly limits its use in terms of verification procedures.

PRIVATE AND UNLISTED COMPANIES

Private and unlisted companies are subject to a lower level of public disclosure than publically quoted companies. The structure, ownership, purpose and activities of private companies will also tend to be clearer and easier for a firm to understand. Furthermore, private companies may be long established reputable organisations with long histories of public information, although others will be young developing businesses, many of which will fail in their first three years.

The regulations which are generally applied state that standard information may be sufficient evidence to meet the firm's obligations. It is also worth searching the company's registry to check that a firm is not in the process of being dissolved, struck off or wound up, but again this is not specifically conducted to identify money laundering. Firms should make search enquiries of the registry in the country of incorporation for the relevant company. The documentation obtained from such searches can be checked as part of the due diligence process. The accessibility of such documentation will vary considerably between different countries and firms should pay particular care when faced with obstacles when verifying company identification. This should raise additional concerns.

In countries where there is less transparency, less of an industry profile, or less independent means of verifying the client identity there is a higher risk of money laundering or terrorist financing. In such cases, in addition to the standard identification procedures set out above, firms should verify the identity of shareholders and controllers and conduct such additional procedures as they consider appropriate in the circumstances. A visit to the place of business may also help to confirm the existence and activities of the entity, as well as other business associations which may influence the firm's operations – although the office may just have been set up to convey the appearance of a business to satisfy the financial institution. One thing to look for is the appearance that everything is very new or that people are not really working. Perhaps undertake a surprise visit unannounced and see if the company looks the same as when the formal arranged meeting took place.

While the rule is generally that directors of companies need not be investigated unless they are also beneficial owners of a company, this is unlikely to be sensible in the case of smaller or private family businesses, trusts or charities. In such cases firms should consider whether the retail identification procedures should in fact be applied to significant individuals within the structure. Any failure to comply with such a request should alert the firm to the enhanced risk that clearly then exists.

The firm should undertake a risk assessment of a firm's money laundering risk to identify which person's identity it is necessary to identify. Verification will normally be appropriate for those officers that have authority to operate an account or to give the firm instructions concerning the use or transfer of funds or assets, but might be waived for other directors.

As is the case with public companies, firms also wish, as part of a risk-based approach, to take adequate measures to verify the identity of beneficial owners (those controlling 25% or more of the company's shares or voting rights), as well as individual signatories. Signatories may also be identified as part of a risk-based approach, due to their power to give instructions concerning the movement of funds or assets, as well as their power to authorise directors to make decisions.

ENHANCED DUE DILIGENCE

Additional enhanced due diligence measures should be undertaken if the nature of the customer, its business, location, and product or delivery channel is assessed under a risk-based approach as needing additional verification. Such measures may include requesting additional identity information.

If a firm is linked in some way to a politically exposed person (PEP) then they are higher risk and should be subject to enhanced due diligence. This is addressed in Chapter 14. If the firm is itself regulated by an active regulator, then this could mean that some form of simplified process on the other hand is appropriate if this is permitted by local rules.

Extra care must also be taken when dealing with companies with capital in the form of bearer shares, because it will inevitably be difficult to identify the beneficial owners. Companies that issue bearer bonds will also typically be incorporated in higher risk jurisdictions since in most countries the practice has died out. Therefore firms should implement procedures to establish the identities of the holders and material beneficial owners of such shares to ensure they are in particular notified of any change in ownership.

As a minimum precaution, firms should obtain an undertaking in writing from the beneficial owner which states that immediate notification will be given to the firm if shares are transferred to another party. Depending on the risk assessment of the customer, it may be appropriate to have this undertaking certified by an accountant or lawyer, or require shares to be held by a custodian, with an undertaking on the custodian to notify the firm of any changes.

CHARITIES AND TRUSTS

These both represent areas with an enhanced risk of money laundering and terrorist financing and therefore generally additional work will need to be undertaken. Here the deeds that formed the organisation will need to be obtained and the objectives verified. As part of the ongoing monitoring of activity the firm should seek to ensure that there is no evidence that the organisation's income and expenditure structure is inconsistent with the stated objectives of the organisation.

They should also seek to verify the controllers of these organisations since in such cases there is rarely a beneficial owner and the original settlors are of relatively limited interest. They may have died centuries earlier.

The UK Charities Commission provides a standard regarding charities potentially financing terrorism. This advice and guidance is relevant to any firm in this space.[1]

The Commission states: "Our approach rests on 3 key principles that we apply when considering charities with potential links to

---

[1]It may be found at: http://www.charity-commission.gov.uk/supportingcharities/ogs/g096.asp.

terrorism." These principles were applied before the events of September 11,2001 and have been applied since. The Commission states that:

1. We would not register an organisation that had support of terrorism as an object.
2. The use of an existing charity's assets for support of terrorist activity is not a proper use of those assets.
3. Any links or alleged links between a charity and terrorism are corrosive to public confidence in the integrity of charity.

The Commission expects trustees to be vigilant to ensure that a charity's premises, assets, volunteers or other goods cannot be used for activities that may, or appear to, support or condone terrorist activities. Examples include the use of a charity's premises for fundraising or meetings.

Further, charities should take all necessary steps to ensure that their activities could not be misinterpreted. The Commission expects trustees of charities to take all necessary steps to ensure that their activities are transparent, for example including transfer of assets abroad. They hold trustees accountable for ensuring that procedures are put in place to ensure that terrorist organisations cannot take advantage of a charity's status, reputation, facilities or assets.

It is however for the firm to assess whether the procedures operated within the trust or charity appear to be adequate to ensure that it is only used for legitimate purposes and it is this area that should be the subject of their attention.

Firms should have clearly documented processes and procedures for dealing with all such cases which need to be rigorously enforced.

Chapter 14

POLITICALLY EXPOSED PERSONS

WHAT IS A POLITICALLY EXPOSED PERSON?

Politically exposed persons (PEPs) are quite simply a high risk category of individuals which are internationally recognised as needing enhanced due diligence requirements. The general concern is that persons that hold high profile political positions and those related or associated with them will pose a higher money laundering risk to firms as their position makes them vulnerable to corruption. The obvious risk is that the politically exposed person may either take some form of facilitation payment to enable a third party to win a contract with government or abscond with government funds. In the United Kingdom the recently enacted Bribery Act brings this into clear focus.

Of course not all PEPs will actually be conducting illegal activity – all that the requirements ask is that the firm undertakes additional procedures commensurate with the level of risk that the relationship poses to the firm. The issue is then to identify PEPs and, as we shall discuss, we would recommend that firms take a broad definition of such relationships. The only risk that is posed to a firm through undertaking analysis on more relationships than the minimum requirements is that some element of unnecessary due diligence will have been conducted – this would not appear to represent a significant waste of resources. It may result in the reputation of the firm being additionally protected.

From the point of view of the financial institution, it is clear that being involved with a politically exposed person will inevitably result in a higher level of public scrutiny and a consequent increased risk of adverse publicity. This would result from public disclosure through newspapers or electronic media of a firm having facilitated an illegal advantage being obtained by a PEP which had been, or should have been, identified by the firm.

The question as to who really is a politically exposed person is a significant issue for any regulated firm. Someone may suddenly become a politically exposed person having been a client of the firm for many years through standing and winning an election. In many countries independents have risen to public office from roles which would not have previously resulted in their being identified as PEPs. Others may be in power and operating entirely legally for many years, only having the opportunity to act illegally at some later stage. They have actually been politically exposed throughout the period, but have only undertaken inappropriate activity when the opportunity presented itself, perhaps just before they leave office. This highlights the importance of continuing to monitor such relationships throughout the period when the customer is identified as a PEP.

Remember that a customer having PEP status does not incriminate the individual in itself; however the status does put such customers into a high risk category. The Third EC Directive, as well as the JMLSG's Guidance notes both particularly identify PEPs as an area of concern in the fight against money laundering. Accordingly regulated firms should have both a clear definition as to who is a PEP and have clearly documented the additional procedures that should be undertaken on PEP transactions. It is incumbent on the firm to be able to demonstrate to their regulators that appropriate and consistent procedures have been conducted, with adequate documentation of these additional procedures being maintained.

THE DEFINITION OF A POLITICALLY EXPOSED PERSON (PEP)

The UK's Money Laundering Regulations define a PEP as:

> *an individual who is or has, at any time in the preceding year, been entrusted with prominently public functions and an immediate family member, or a known close associate, of such a person.*

The UK's definition applies to those holding such a position in a state outside the UK, or in a Community institution or an international body. This is actually quite a limited statement. It means, for example, that someone that stands for public office but loses in an election would not be a PEP within the definition of the term. However many firms will actually use a wider definition, which we would recommend. This bases itself on the firm's ability to know who can significantly influence functions of importance, regardless of whether or not they are entrusted with a public function. It is often the person that has influence that can be the person most easily bribed.

There is also a limitation in the UK definition in that an individual ceases to be recognised as a PEP after they have left office for one year. There is clearly an argument that such a time limit is far too short since the individual would clearly remain high profile even if they are no longer a public official. Consider the position of former US Presidents or UK prime ministers, for example. The way that the UK rules operate to deal with this is in part by encouraging the implementation of a risk-based approach. This is a series of policies and procedures implemented in the firm that enables the firm to identify what might be considered as higher risk relationships, regardless of whether they are or are not PEPs. All PEPs are by definition higher risk relationships, but not all higher risk relationships are in fact PEPs. All higher risk relationships will require enhanced due diligence and continual monitoring and we would recommend that former officials should be regularly reviewed until such time as their ability to influence has waned to such an extent that it is inconceivable that they might be undertaking illegal, or at best inappropriate, activity.

An example of this is the recent case of the Duchess of York, the former wife of Prince Andrew, who was recorded by a newspaper as offering access to Prince Andrew in exchange for a cash payment. She claimed that any payment to her would be repaid tenfold through access to her ex-husband who works as a UK trade envoy. Prince Andrew was not in any way implicated by the disclosure. This highlights that someone who in this case is divorced from a person holding a high profile position remains a PEP regardless of the rules and in this case clearly requires enhanced due diligence.

It would make no sense for a firm to cease conducting additional enhanced monitoring of transactions or activity at the end of an additional one-year period. The main consideration that the firm should take into account is whether the risks associated with an individual's previous position have adequately abated, or whether they do in fact continue. This may need to be considered on a case-by-case basis, as opposed to one generic approach. The idea is that regardless of the rules that apply locally, the firm would wish to know that the account that they are maintaining is not being operated inappropriately such that at some time in the future their reputation could be impacted.

AT WHAT LEVEL IS SOMEONE A PEP?

It is generally recognised that public functions that are exercised at a lower than national level should not normally be considered to be prominent. However, there can be cases where people who hold such positions may experience political exposure which is comparable to that of persons with similar positions at national level. An example of this could well be the Mayor of a large city such as London or Paris. As you move towards local politicians of lesser importance then the firm will need to judge whether they could be involved in inappropriate activity and whether such activity could be of such importance that the person should have been considered as a PEP and subject to enhanced monitoring procedures.

Given the number of cases where inappropriate, or at best dubious, payments have been made to officials involved in local planning decisions, the firm may well choose to include all such officials into the enhanced due diligence regime. Of course fraud does not need to be conducted at the most senior level. In a 2009 case in Toronto, Canada, nine city staff were removed from office on suspicion of scamming employee benefits and faced a police investigation after a report revealed more than $500 000 in potential fraud by city staff and contractors.

Examples of abuse included an employee who claimed $50 000 worth of unwarranted overtime, another who cancelled parking tickets for friends and family, and two members of staff who used counterfeit passes to take advantage of $550 worth of recreational programming. "I guess there's people out there who think of themselves first and are willing to perpetrate these frauds," said Councillor Doug Holyday. Nine employees were also being investigated for making false claims to the employee benefits plan. Those "irregularities" were flagged by the city's insurance administrator. "I've been saying for years corruption is rampant at City Hall," said Councillor Rob Ford.

A notoriously outspoken watchdog, he said he deals with two to three complaints a week from employees so "petrified" of retribution that he has to meet them in suburban doughnut shops or in vehicles going through a car wash.

This highlights that fraud can clearly operate at all levels of a firm, but for a really high level case to result in adverse publicity the culprit would need to be at a senior level. In this case the issues were identified by the financial institution acting as administrator which shows that they at least were undertaking due diligence on all such cases.

Once again the key requirement will be for firms to implement a risk-based approach, using some form of consistent modelling and criteria to establish whether persons exercising those public functions should be considered as PEPs. We would recommend that a standard scoring system be implemented which sets key attributes for the identification of a PEP, with weighted scoring then applied. This will enable consistent application of relevant due diligence approaches to be undertaken and provide the necessary supporting evidence to justify the approach adopted. Of course a scoring system will not replace judgement. Instead it provides a structure within which judgement can be consistently applied, justified and adequately documented.

PROMINENT PUBLIC FUNCTIONS

The UK Regulations state that prominent public functions include:

- heads of state, heads of government, ministers, and deputy or assistant ministers;
- Members of Parliament;
- members of supreme courts, constitutional courts or other higher level judicial bodies;
- members of courts of auditors or of the boards of central banks;
- ambassadors, chargés d'affaires and high ranking officers in the armed forces;
- members of the administrative, management or supervisory boards of state-owned enterprises.

As such these are pretty typical of the rules that are implemented globally.

We can take as an example a recent case from South Africa, reported on 26 November 2009, in which 923 government officials were caught for undertaking fraud.

Of those arrested, 800 were from national and provincial government and 123 from local government. Five members of the legal fraternity had also been struck off the roll for housing corruption. In this case 40000 houses across the country were demolished or had to be rectified because of poor workmanship. Two of these collapsed, causing the deaths of a 13-year-old boy and a woman. The situation followed from questionable contracts and building standards approved by government officials and implemented by the private sector.

This case clearly illustrates that local and provincial government officials can all be involved in inappropriate activity through the receiving of inappropriate payments (or graft). The laundering of such proceeds through bank accounts without the bank having considered whether they were legally earned could potentially lay the banks open to the risk of being caught within a money laundering investigation.

It is therefore clear that regardless of the actual rules that have been implemented, in cases where the relationship results in additional levels of risk, the bank should undertake procedures which are commensurate with this potential risk. What this is likely to mean in practice is that the bank will analyse its relationships into four distinct groups:

- PEP accounts as defined by the local rules and regulations;
- accounts which represent an enhanced risk of inappropriate activity;
- other accounts, considered as standard risk;
- accounts considered by the local rules and regulations as being low risk.

In these terms a low risk account could, for example, be an account set up by an employer purely for the salary of an employee.

Of course not all inappropriate conduct will be identifiable by a financial institution. In public officials relatively small amounts of inappropriate activity can result in adverse publicity for the person involved. The series of revelations regarding UK MPs' expenses in 2009 represent a clear case of such items. For example, a five-foot tall floating duck house was claimed from the public purse by Tory grandee Sir Peter Viggers. The £1645 pond feature, modelled on an 18th century Swedish building by a firm selling elaborate garden follies, sits in the pond at the Gosport MP's Hampshire home. Clearly a single payment of £1645 would be unlikely to be identified by a financial institution. Claims by other MPs included submissions for jellied eels, fluffy dusters and horse manure. It would be unreasonable to expect all cases of inappropriate conduct by government officials to be identified by financial institutions.

THE IMMEDIATE FAMILY RULES

Generally the rules applied will require that the immediate family members of a PEP are also included with the PEP in the additional monitoring regime. In the UK this is required, but in other countries it may be difficult or legally impossible to consider such connections. The issue is again clear – it may well be that the PEP transfers the inappropriate funds to a family member rather than taking it directly, or that the family member is able to exert undue influence on the PEP. There could of course be cases where the PEP undertakes inappropriate conduct but asks for the facilitation payment to be made to their spouse or children. In such cases it will only become apparent through monitoring the spouse or child's account.

When it is possible to undertake such monitoring the definition of immediate family members generally includes:

- a spouse;
- a partner (including a person who is considered by his national law as equivalent to a spouse);
- children and their spouses and partners;
- parents.

What it does not generally include are brothers and sisters, nor any more remote members of the same family. Whether a firm would wish to extend the definition of family to people beyond this list is, of course, purely a matter for the individual firm to consider. By complying with the local requirements they will have met the regulator's expectations. However they may choose to undertake additional procedures on a wider group of people due to the risks that they pose to the institution itself.

THE ASSOCIATE RULES

It is normally also important to include the associate of a PEP when considering enhanced money laundering deterrence procedures. These requirements are intended to identify people with a close business relationship to a PEP that might potentially also be involved in inappropriate activity due to their relationship with, for example, a local official. A firm will need to define clearly what constitutes an associate, using a definition that includes anything that is within the local regulatory definition. Such definitions will typically include the following:

- any individual who is known to have joint beneficial ownership of a legal entity, or any other close business relations with a person who is a PEP;
- any individual who has sole beneficial ownership of a legal entity which is known to have been set up for the benefit of a person who is a PEP.

In determining whether a person is an associate of a PEP, the firm generally only needs to consider any information which is in its possession, or which is publicly known. It does not have to go out of its way to find out additional nonpublic information. Therefore the obligation of having to obtain knowledge of such a relationship does not presuppose that active research should be conducted by the firm.

Again the firm should implement a risk-based approach in determining associates of PEPs, and the enhanced due diligence measures which should then be conducted. If there is a known associate who is not actually a joint owner of anything with the PEP, then it would still be wise for the firm to consider them as an associate. It is to such relationships that the PEP might turn to undertake illegal activity or for them to receive illicit funds on their behalf and therefore disguise their original source.

A recent example of the involvement of associates in an official's fraudulent activities is a February 2010 UK case. This represented a complex fraud which left Yorkshire council tax payers with a bill of £13.6m. Three men involved in the scam were given suspended sentences and ordered to pay back the cash they made.

Three businessmen pleaded guilty to conspiracy to commit false accounting. The fraud at South Yorkshire Trading Standards Unit, known as SYTSU, lasted almost five years. The unit was run by Mike Buckley, who was globally renowned as an expert in his field, and who, Sheffield Crown Court heard, was motivated by his vanity. The scale of the scheme only became clear after his death. Buckley had a reputation as an international expert in metrology, the science of calibrating weighing equipment, but he had in fact been running SYTSU dishonestly. An investigation after his death in 2005 revealed he had "embarked on a course of conduct which was directed towards his own personal aggrandisement".

He used deals with the three businessmen to make false representations about his unit's income to make him look more successful. Buckley set up agreements with them to supply falsely inflated invoices to SYTSU relating to the supply of calibration equipment. Buckley paid the invoices from SYTSU cash but then conspired with the defendants in an arrangement which saw them pay an invoice raised by his unit for nonexistent "calibration work".

Barristers for each of the three defendants said they were ashamed of what had happened and had initially trusted Buckley and his reputation when he asked them to produce "unusual" invoices.

Here it is clear that the business associates were instrumental in the fraudulent activity and therefore should clearly have been identified and monitored, were it clear to the financial institution that they were actually associates of the official. It is the difficulty in knowing the total extent of an official's associates which lies at the heart of the problems that a firm is likely to face in practice. All that a firm can do is conduct a standard set of documented procedures which attempt to undertake the investigations that a relatively diligent institution would be expected to conduct, and to maintain sufficient records to justify any decisions taken.

WHAT IS THE RISK-BASED APPROACH?

There is no single definition of what constitutes the risk-based approach and firms will need to consider their own local circumstances in developing appropriate criteria to apply in practice. Actual identified cases of PEPs being involved with local money laundering or terrorist financing can be used to back test any criteria that have been developed. This is done by taking cases of known money laundering and then applying the criteria adopted within the firm's documented enhanced due diligence procedures. They should be able to see if the case would have been identified by their systems as one requiring enhanced monitoring.

Generally the requirement here is for the firm to develop a series of policies and procedures to ensure that the firm:

- has appropriate risk-based procedures to determine whether a customer is a PEP;
- obtains appropriate senior management approval for establishing a business relationship with a customer;
- takes adequate measures to establish the source of wealth and source of funds which are involved in the business relationship or occasional transaction;
- conducts enhanced ongoing monitoring of the business relationship.

THE RISK-BASED APPROACH TO DETERMINING PEPs

The extent to which PEPs themselves affect a firm's money laundering obligations will depend on the nature and scope of the firm's business and whether the PEP would have a significant impact on the public perception or reputation of the firm were a case of money laundering or terrorist financing to be identified.

When applying a risk-based approach, it would be appropriate for the firm's resources to be focused on particular products or transactions which are characterised by a high risk of money laundering. This will be determined through knowledge of money laundering transactions that are generally conducted within the local jurisdiction and would typically, for example, focus on cash-based and non face-to-face transactions.

Firms will first have to identify whether a PEP exists as part of its customer base. When applying specific checks firms may be able to rely on an internet search engine, or consult relevant reports and databases regarding public officials. There are also corruption risk indices published by specialised national, international, non-governmental and commercial organisations. The Transparency International Corruption Perceptions Index, for example, ranks approximately 150 countries according to their perceived level of corruption. Clearly such an index helps firms in assessing risk since a politician from a high risk country would clearly need to receive enhanced monitoring procedures.

It is also important to remember that whilst new and existing customers may not meet the definition of a PEP, they may subsequently become one during the course of the business relationship. In this respect, firms must, as far as is practically possible, be alert to public information regarding the possible changes in the status of their customers with regard to political exposure. In practice this will mean conducting reviews on a regular basis to see if the PEPs identified are in fact a complete population of such accounts, or whether an existing customer has become a PEP and should now be subject to enhanced monitoring. After an election for office it is clear that an additional review should be conducted to identify newly elected PEPs who would now require additional monitoring.

The identification of the PEP, family member or associate is only the first stage in the process. Once a PEP has been identified firms must then be clear as to the enhanced due diligence procedures that they should conduct in order to minimise where possible their risk of being involved with an account which actually constitutes money laundering or terrorist financing.

TRANSPARENCY INTERNATIONAL

Transparency International is an international organisation that works to fight against corruption and produces an annual Global Corruption Report, The Transparency International Corruption Perceptions Index. The current list is included as an annex to this book.

Transparency International provides a series of clear definitions that should prove to be of assistance to people drafting money laundering deterrence or terrorist financing policies. Within these definitions, Transparency International specifically defines political corruption and the problems involved with it are explained in depth. Political corruption is defined as the abuse of entrusted power by political leaders for private gain, with the objective of increasing power or wealth. It does not need to involve money changing hands; it may take the form of "trading in influence" or granting favours for the intention of receiving benefit.

Political corruption involves a wide range of crimes and illicit acts committed by political leaders before, during and after leaving office. It is distinct from petty or bureaucratic corruption in so far as it is perpetrated by political leaders or elected officials who have been vested with public authority and who bear the responsibility of representing the public interest. There is also a supply side to political corruption – the bribes paid to politicians – that must be addressed.

Business people also sense the effects of political corruption. A survey by the World Economic Forum shows that business people believe that legal donations have a high impact on politics, that bribery does feature as a regular means of achieving policy goals in about 20% of countries surveyed, and that illegal political contributions are standard practice in nearly half of all countries surveyed. Political corruption points to a lack of transparency, but also to related concerns about equity and justice: corruption feeds the wrongs that deny human rights and prevent human needs from being met.

Transparency International also publishes a bribe payer's index, an example of which is shown in Table 14.1.

Table 14.1 Bribe Payers Index 2008

Rank	Country/ Territory	BPI 2008 Score	Standard Deviation	Confidence Interval 95% Lower Bound	Confidence Interval 95% Upper Bound
1	Belgium	8,8	2,00	8,5	9,0
1	Canada	8,8	1,80	8,5	9,0
3	Netherlands	8,7	1,98	8,4	8,9
3	Switzerland	8,7	1,98	8,4	8,9
5	Germany	8,6	2,14	8,4	8,8
5	Japan	8,6	2,11	8,3	8,8
5	United Kingdom	8,6	2,10	8,4	8,7
8	Australia	8,5	2,23	9,2	8,7
9	France	8,1	2,48	7,9	8,3
9	Singapore	8,1	2,60	7,8	8,4
9	United States	8,1	2,43	7,9	8,3
12	Spain	7,9	2,49	7,6	8,1
13	Hong Kong	7,6	2,67	7,3	7,9
14	South Africa	7,5	2,78	7,1	8,0
14	South Korea	7,5	2,79	7,1	7,8
14	Taiwan	7,5	2,76	7,1	7,8
17	Brazil	7,4	2,78	7,0	7,7
17	Italy	7,4	2,89	7,1	7,7
19	India	6,8	3,31	6,4	7,3
20	Mexico	6,6	2,97	6,1	7,2
21	China	6,5	3,35	6,2	6,8
22	Russia	5,9	3,66	5,2	6,6

Source: Transparency International Bribe Payers Survey 2008.
Scores range from 0 to 10. The higher the score for the country, the lower the likelihood of companies from this country to engage in bribery when doing business abroad.
For number of observations see Annex.

Again this list may be of benefit to firms in developing risk-based criteria. As you can see the bribes are paid by people in countries which you might consider as being relatively well regulated. It is the countries that are poorly regulated which are the recipients of such funds.

Chapter 15

NON FACE-TO-FACE CUSTOMERS

WHO ARE NON FACE-TO-FACE CUSTOMERS?

A non face-to-face transaction is one that occurs without a customer having to be physically present. Examples of this type of activity include internet banking, telephone banking, credit cards and online share dealing. Non face-to-face business is becoming increasingly popular in the financial services industry due to increased customer demand and the high costs of maintaining personal customer contact services; the ability to transact from a distance has been facilitated by developments in technology and telecommunications.

It is generally agreed that non face-to-face transactions are more risky than face-to-face transactions since the primary identification measures which must be carried out cannot include matching the face of the customer with a document. To overcome this in some countries it is commonplace for there to be requirements for the customer to visit a branch to have their identity confirmed. However in many countries this is not the case and the financial institution will need to assess the level of risk that the relationship poses to the firm in deciding which procedures to adopt.

Clearly, it is still possible, even with a customer facing transaction, for identification fraud to be perpetrated. Much of the identification work is designed to link the person that is in front of the firm's employee with some form of official identification documentation which includes the customer's face. This does not actually prove that the customer is as expected, rather only that the person appearing for identification is the same as the picture that appears on the official document, which might itself be forged.

However, non face-to-face transactions aggravate the risks involved in financial transactions in a number of ways. Firstly the financial institution actually will never have met the customer. Not only would they not know what the customer looked like, but they would also not generally have received official documents that confirm the picture of the customer and link this to the address, date of birth and other relevant details. This is due to the unwillingness of customers to part with such high risk documents to send them to a remote location.

The following factors all contribute to the additional risks that are involved in a firm undertaking business with customers on a non face-to-face basis:

- The ease by which the customer will have access to the facility, regardless of time and location, with a minimum of controls in operation.
- The ease of making multiple fictitious applications without the customer incurring extra costs or there being a significant risk of detection by the firm.
- The absence of physical documents. This is not only the absence of any identification documents, but also the absence of signed contractual documentation; although some firms do request that documents should be signed and posted back. The firm, of course, has no way of verifying the signature!
- The speed at which electronic transactions are undertaken also renders it difficult to verify data prior to a transaction being committed to. Controls generally only operate in arrears and would have the effect of recording the inappropriate transaction.

ADDITIONAL MEASURES FOR NON FACE-TO-FACE CUSTOMERS

Any firm that is engaged in non face-to-face business activity will need to develop a series of appropriate risk-based policies and procedures to ensure that adequate controls are actually applied in practice. The nature of such additional procedures as are required will of course vary depending on the nature and scope of the non face-to-face activities. The type of issues that a firm should consider will include the following:

- The firm still needs to think about how it will identify the customer. This may involve receiving some form of documentation or taking additional steps seeking independent data for verification. At the very least if taking a deposit they will need to think how they would be able to provide the funds back to the customer in the absence of robust identification procedures having been conducted.
- The nature of supplementary measures to verify or certify the documents supplied or requiring confirmatory certification will also vary depending on the jurisdiction. There may be independent data that serves this purpose, for example electoral roll data or credit reference agency search information. It is the combination of data from various sources which potentially provides the required level of additional assurance.

- The firm will undertake work to consider the nature of the payment profile of the customer. Typically they will require the first payment resulting from the operation of the account to be carried out through an account opened in the customer's name with a prime bank. The non face-to-face firm is thereby trying to gain some level of assurance from the work conducted by a firm that does maintain a face-to-face relationship with the client. In doing this the bank will need to assess whether they are satisfied with the quality of the bank in which the account is placed and many restrict such activity to a bank based in their own jurisdiction which is known to maintain high quality controls.

RISK-BASED APPROACH TO NON FACE-TO-FACE CUSTOMERS

The extent to which additional money laundering deterrence measures need to be carried out should be judged through the application of the risk-based approach. The extent of verification that will actually be conducted will therefore depend on the nature and characteristics of the product or service requested and the firm's assessment of the money laundering risk presented by the customer.

While we have so far concentrated on retail customers you do need to recognise that in some parts of the industry it is normal for the customer not to be present – in wholesale markets for example. In such cases the focus needs to be on identifying that the financial institution is the firm that it purports to be and that the officer has the authority to bind the firm. Again it is necessary to ensure that the named subsidiary of a bank is actually known by the holding company, since this has been abused in a number of cases. Whilst additional procedures are implemented, such circumstances do not in themselves increase the risk of money laundering in a transaction. Therefore, firms need to be able to judge for themselves which transactions appear to represent a higher risk of money laundering or terrorist financing and develop appropriate systems and procedures to enable them to do this.

One particular additional area of concern is customers that appear to be deliberately avoiding face-to-face contact. If such a scenario were to occur, it would be advisable for firms to have a clear and appropriate policy that deals with such circumstances, particularly systems and procedures as mentioned above. We would generally recommend that any such cases should be rejected and the customer potentially reported to the relevant authority.

The problems of buying online

Sir Tim Berners-Lee, who invented the world wide web 20 years ago, was actually conned online himself. In 2009 he reported that he had bought a Christmas present from an online shop. It was only when the present didn't arrive that he realised he had been conned.

He is one of an increasing number of victims of online cyber crime. Around one in four internet users in the UK have fallen victim to online phishing scams that attempt to steal people's financial details while one in six have fallen victim to other types of online fraud:

> *The worst thing that has happened to me was when I tried to buy a Christmas present from a company that looked like a bona fide company on the internet and then actually they were a completely fake company. I think I am yet to get the money back, but it wasn't a lot. The moment I called the 0800 number listed on the website, there was a very polite message saying this number is available if you would like to use it, so a little bit of due diligence on my part would have revealed it wasn't what it was set up to be.*

This again highlights that just by doing some basic due diligence procedures and attempting to really know your customer then you may be able to identify the illegal transaction. In this case some financial institution would have been banking and transferring the sums resulting from the fraudulent site, which would clearly be caught by the Regulations. Consequently it is also incumbent upon firms to take care in monitoring the activity of any company who undertakes a high level of online trading in case they are also operating illegally.

Chapter 16

SUSPICIOUS CONDUCT AND TRANSACTIONS

INTRODUCTION

What is suspicious activity? The problem is that it is easy to see with hindsight – but are there signals that can be identified in advance? Both society at large and regulators are increasingly expecting a firm to have adequate procedures to detect suspicious activity. Many regulators actually publish lists of transactions that they consider are such that they should result in a firm becoming suspicious, but these can only ever be a subset of the type of transactions that are likely to be of concern in practice. The problem is that the expectation being placed on financial institutions may well exceed their ability to identify suspicious transactions.

Identifying, investigating and documenting a suspicion is always a problem for a bank. If an employee becomes suspicious regarding a particular transaction then the firm is clearly under an obligation to undertake a review to establish whether there are actually grounds for a true suspicion and that consequent suspicious activity reporting (SAR) is necessary. The process adopted needs to be formally documented with the reason for reporting, or not reporting, the transaction being clearly set out. It may be necessary to provide protection to the bank in future potential legal actions against claims that they have failed to do what was required of them. The investigation needs to be conducted without the customer becoming aware that a potential review into a possible case of money laundering is being undertaken since this would fall within the definition of tipping off (Chapter 20).

If there definitely is a suspicion then the position is even worse. Nothing can be done that would in any way cause the customer to consider that they might be the subject of a SAR, since this again would represent tipping off, which is a criminal offence in most countries. However there is an obligation under most regulations to make full and complete disclosure. Accordingly great care needs to be taken to make sure that all actions are appropriate and consistent with the legislation.

WHAT IS A SUSPICIOUS TRANSACTION?

The following are examples of potentially suspicious activities that might raise initial concerns. They would therefore indicate that the transactions are worthy of further investigation to determine whether the transactions or activities reflect illicit activities rather than legitimate business activities and whether a SAR should be filed.

ACTIVITY INCONSISTENT WITH THE CUSTOMER'S BUSINESS

- A customer opens a greater number of different accounts than would be expected for the type of business they are purportedly conducting and/or frequently transfers funds among those accounts.
- A customer's corporate account(s) has deposits or withdrawals primarily in cash rather than cheques or other types of transfer.
- When a bank expects a customer to want cash given the nature of their activity and the customer fails to make such a request then this will also cause concerns. For example, the owner of both a retail business and a cheque cashing service that does not ask for cash when depositing cheques, will possibly indicate the availability of another source of cash, which could of course be illegitimate.
- Any unusual pattern of cash transactions will alert the bank to potential concerns. If the customer engages in unusual activity in cash purchases of traveller's cheques, money orders or cashier's cheques then this is likely to be an area requiring investigation.
- Activity that is inconsistent with the bank's understanding of the customer will always be a cause for concern. For example if a customer deposits a large volume of cashier's cheques, money orders, and/or wire transfers into an account when the nature of the account holder's business would not appear to justify such activity, then further reviews would be required.
- Generally if a customer frequently makes large dollar transactions (such as deposits, withdrawals or purchases of monetary instruments) without an explanation as to how they will be used in the business, or the purchases allegedly are for a business that generally does not deal in large amounts of cash, then investigation will be required.
- If there is a business account history that shows little or no regular, periodic activity, or the account appears to be used primarily as a temporary repository for funds that are transferred abroad then this will be considered as high risk. For example, if the account has numerous deposits of cash which are then

followed by a single lump-sum wire transfer overseas then this could be disguising drug trafficking.

- The bank should always wonder why the account has been brought to them. Accordingly if a customer's place of business or residence is outside the financial institution's normal service area then this is likely to raise concerns and require enhanced due diligence to be conducted.
- Understanding your customer is paramount and there cannot be any replacement for such analysis. What is unusual will need to be judged against the nature of the activity conducted. For many firms a corporate customer that frequently makes large cash deposits and maintains high balances but does not use other banking services would alert the firm to the need to do additional investigation.
- Similarly a retail business that routinely makes numerous deposits of cheques, but rarely makes cash withdrawals for daily operations would appear to be unusual activity. Likewise a retail business that has dramatically different patterns of cash deposits from similar businesses in the same general location might indicate that matters are not quite what they seem.
- In terms of layering of money laundering this may arise from an international transfer in an unusual currency. Generally if the currency transaction patterns of a business experience a sudden and inconsistent change from normal activities it would be expected that this would be identified by the firm and reviews conducted.
- For customers where there is a high level of knowledge it may be possible that even greater levels of identification could be undertaken. For example, if the amount and frequency of cash deposits are inconsistent with that observed at the customer's place of business then this might alert the firm to some concern. Similarly if the business frequently deposits large amounts of cash, but cheques or other debits drawn against the account are inconsistent with the customer's retail business then this should be checked out.
- If a business that does not normally generate overseas currency suddenly starts to make numerous currency transactions (e.g., a sanitation company that makes numerous deposits of cash) then this should be identified and reviewed.
- Sometimes criminals will try to identify a weakness in a control environment which they are able to exploit to disguise their activities. Accordingly financial transactions involving monetary instruments that are either incomplete or contain fictitious payees, remitters, etc., if known, will be a particular concern.

- Generally transactions which do not appear to have a commercial basis will be a cause for concern. For example, unusual transfers of funds among related accounts or accounts that involve the same principal or related principals should be investigated.
- If a business owner, such as an owner who has only one store, makes several deposits the same day using different bank branches then this will be highly unusual. However if the same customer uses accounts at a number of different banks then they would be unlikely to be identified.

AVOIDING A NATIONAL REPORTING OR RECORD-KEEPING REQUIREMENT

If transactions look as if they are being organised to try to avoid a record-keeping or reporting requirement then this should also be a cause for potential concern. Even though there may be good commercial reasons for such activity, a higher level of investigation will be required. These requirements may be national, regulatory or generated by the policies and procedures of the institution concerned. All that is required is that they have been brought to the attention of the potential criminal.

Typical examples of transactions that might cause concern and warrant additional investigation include the following:

- Any business or new customer that asks to be exempted from policies or procedures, which are generally known in the market or are required by rules and regulations, would clearly provide reasons for investigation.
- A customer that intentionally appears to withhold part of a currency deposit or withdrawal to keep the transaction under the reporting threshold should be identified by software designed for this purpose. It suggests that the customer is aware of a reporting threshold and is attempting to avoid detection by acting below it.
- If a customer is reluctant to provide the information needed to file any form of mandatory report, to have the report filed or to proceed with a transaction after being informed that the report must be filed, then there is unlikely to be an innocent reason for this. Accordingly such accounts should be investigated.
- Similarly if a customer or group tries to coerce a bank employee into not filing any required record-keeping or reporting forms

then this should immediately ring alarm bells and would require investigation.

- The customer may try to avoid face-to-face contact to avoid detection. Consequently if a customer uses an automatic teller machine or machines (ATM) to make several bank deposits or withdrawals just below a specified threshold, then this would be cause for concern.
- Failure to provide an identification document that should be easily available will also raise a concern. For example, a customer that is reluctant to furnish identification when purchasing negotiable instruments in significant amounts would obviously represent an account worthy of investigation.

This is of course just a small subset of the type of of transactions that might give rise to concerns and each firm needs to produce a list to set out what might be appropriate in their specific circumstances. This needs to be tailored to the specific needs of the business and to be as relevant as possible such that staff would both understand the issue and know what to do.

WIRE OR FUND TRANSFERS

Any transaction that reduces the level of review that can be undertaken prior to a transaction actually taking place and funds being transferred must be a cause for additional concern to a financial institution. Clearly wiring of fund transfers falls into this category due to the speed with which such funds can be transferred to a third party and moved around the system. Increasingly regulators have become concerned with such transactions, which form part of the layering process within the money laundering landscape.

In this area examples of transactions that might create concerns and warrant additional investigation include the following:

- Wire transfer activity to/from financial secrecy haven countries without an apparent business reason or when it is inconsistent with the customer's business or history. Recognise that such havens may be used legitimately as part of taxation or estate planning and therefore it is important to understand the nature of the customer's business in such cases.
- Periodic wire transfers from a personal account(s) to bank secrecy haven countries may also be indicative of inappropriate conduct, with taxation evasion perhaps being a prime cause. However again estate and legitimate taxation planning could also be

involved, so not all such cases will actually result in confirmed suspicions.

- Large incoming wire transfers on behalf of a foreign client with little or no explicit reason will need investigation. Diligent clients notify their bank in advance if any such case occurs, but many will fail to do so. Attempting to obtain necessary information may prove difficult in such cases and the risk of tipping off is enhanced.
- Large, round transaction amounts, for example \$1m or £500 000 may also be a concern unless it is known that the client regularly does business in such amounts.
- Funds transferred in and out of an account on the same day or within a relatively short period of time (say five working days) should be reported by relevant software systems. It might suggest that money laundering layering is taking place, although it may also suggest that the customer is using another bank for other purposes.
- Payments or receipts with no apparent links to legitimate contracts, goods or services would obviously be a concern. For example if a UK retailer suddenly made a large deposit in rands then you would expect suspicions to be alerted.
- Transfers routed through multiple foreign or domestic banks without any obvious reason would again suggest that money laundering layering was being conducted.
- Likewise unexplained repetitive or unusual patterns of activity should be investigated, again without alerting the client to the nature of the investigation. Using customer relationship management techniques may elicit the required information, suggesting that the fees may have been unduly high and enabling greater information to be obtained.
- Deposits of funds into several accounts, usually in relatively small but regular amounts, which are consolidated subsequently into one master account and transferred, often outside the country, should alert the firm to suspicion. There could be legitimate reasons, for example a newspaper vendor with family overseas. However this could be retail drug vending with money laundering layering following which would warrant investigation.
- Instructions to a financial institution to wire transfer funds abroad and to expect an incoming wire transfer of funds (in an equal amount) from other sources again might be warning the firm of layering. It could also be that inappropriate payments are being made to third parties and being reimbursed, which at the very least might represent reputational risk.

- Regular deposits or withdrawals of large amounts of cash, using wire transfers to, from or through countries that either are known sources of narcotics or whose laws are ineffective in controlling the laundering of money would obviously need to be investigated.

INSUFFICIENT OR SUSPICIOUS INFORMATION BY CUSTOMER

It may well be that the customer, in providing the data requested by the financial institution, inadvertently creates a form of suspicion. There may be a reliance on data which make little or no apparent sense given the nature of the activity conducted by the customer, or a reluctance to provide certain information. Recognise that the customer's reluctance may be natural concern that the data is unnecessary for the bank's purpose and might lead to more marketing, rather than criminal activity. Further it also needs to be recognised that a high quality money launderer always has the best quality documentation, so absence of documentation rarely catches money laundering.

However there are signs that might give rise to concern and should be identified by the financial institution. These include the following:

- The reluctance of a business that is establishing a new account to provide complete information about the purpose of business, its prior banking relationships, names of its officers and directors, and information about the location of the business.
- A customer's refusal to provide the usual information necessary to qualify for credit or other banking services.
- A spike in the customer's activity with little or no explanation.
- A customer's desire to open an account without providing references, a local address or adequate identification as required by market practice or local legislation or regulation; or refusal to provide any other information the financial institution requires to open an account.
- Unusual or suspicious identification documents that the financial institution cannot readily verify.
- The discovery that a customer's home/business phone is disconnected.

- No record of past or present employment on a loan application.
- A customer makes frequent or large transactions and has no record of past or present employment experience.
- The customer's background is at variance with his or her business activities.
- The customer's financial statements differ from those of similar businesses.

Of course each of these may actually be legitimate and alone may not be sufficient to raise a concern. However collectively or in combination given the nature of the customer's business or activity they may provide causes for greater investigation to be undertaken.

OTHER SUSPICIOUS CUSTOMER ACTIVITY

Suspicion is always difficult to define. Effectively the institution will generally know it when it happens, but the following is a summary list of issues which might at least provide sufficient evidence to warrant some additional level of investigation.

- Substantial deposit(s) of high denomination paper money.
- Mailing address outside the normal jurisdiction or business area of the institution.
- Frequent exchanges of small currency amounts for larger denominations.
- Certificate(s) of deposit or other investment vehicle used as loan collateral.
- A large loan is suddenly paid down with no reasonable explanation of the source of funds.
- Frequent deposits of large amounts of currency wrapped in currency straps that have been stamped by other banks.
- Frequent deposits of currency wrapped in currency straps or currency wrapped in rubber bands that are disorganised and do not balance when counted.
- Frequent deposits of musty or extremely dirty bills.
- A customer who purchases cashier's cheques, money orders and other monetary instruments with large amounts of cash.
- A professional service provider, such as a lawyer, accountant or broker, who makes substantial deposits of cash into client accounts or in-house company accounts, such as trust accounts and escrow accounts.

- A customer insists on meeting bank personnel at a location other than their place of business.
- Domestic bank accounts opened in the name of a *casa de cambio* (money exchange house), followed by suspicious wire transfers and/or structured deposits (under a specified threshold) into these accounts.
- Suspicious movements of funds from one bank into another bank and back into the first bank.
- Offshore companies, especially those located in bank secrecy haven countries, asking for a loan from a domestic bank, or for a loan secured by obligations of offshore banks.
- Use of loan proceeds in a manner inconsistent with the stated loan purpose.
- A person or business that does not hold an account and that purchases a monetary instrument with large denominated bills.
- A customer who purchases a number of cashier's cheques, money orders or traveller's cheques for large amounts under a specified threshold, or without apparent reason.
- Couriers, rather than personal account customers, make the deposits into the account.
- Money orders deposited by mail, which are numbered sequentially or have unusual symbols or stamps on them.

Of course there could easily be a legitimate reason for each of the transactions – we are not suggesting that they *would* be money laundering, rather that they *could* be money laundering. This would always mean that additional review processes should be conducted.

These clearly can only represent a small sample of the type of transactions that might provide a financial institution with cause for concern. What is important is for the firm to make sure that their staff are aware of the type of things they should look out for and for them then to know the actions to be taken in such circumstances. There is clearly a requirement for consistency throughout the banking business, regardless of the nature of activity being conducted. There is little point in a financial institution effectively moving the money launderer from an area where there are high levels of control operating to another area where the controls are perhaps of a lower quality.

There is also the requirement that adequate documentation should be maintained by the firm at a level consistent with the local rules and regulations, together with any group rules. This is both to meet the supervisory requirements and also to support any future investigation to be conducted.

Generally financial institutions will make use of some form of software to provide the analysis that they require. Typical software will select a number of these potential transactions and then codify them into specific scenarios that can be generally applied. Accordingly the codification of the scenario needs to be sufficiently detailed to ensure that the correct transactions are identified and the minimum number of transactions selected for investigation, which eventually are found to not create a suspicion (so called false positives). A suite of scenarios is therefore required which will need to be back tested to see if, had they been in existence at that time, they would have actually identified true cases of money laundering of which the institution is aware.

There needs to be a regular review of all such scenarios to see that they are complete and continue to meet the ongoing needs of the business. It needs to be recognised that money launderers tend to be highly sophisticated and will take advantage of new products that may provide opportunities for money laundering prior to the institution instigating additional money laundering controls in such areas. The skills of the quality money launderer should never be underestimated; therefore a regular and at least annual review of the adequacy of scenarios does need to take place.

Chapter 17

UNUSUAL TRANSACTIONS

THE IDENTIFICATION OF UNUSUAL TRANSACTIONS

Regulations make it clear that staff will be held accountable if they fail to recognise an unusual transaction or arrangement where they have reasonable grounds to know or suspect money laundering activity. This means that there will always need to be clarity and training for staff to enable them to both understand their obligations and also to make sure that they conduct the procedures expected of them in an appropriate way.

Each firm will need to provide clear guidance to all of its employees to enable them to detect those unusual transactions which they are required to identify, or which pose a reputational risk to the firm. Again you need to recognise that the identification of an unusual transaction would not in itself necessarily mean that money laundering or terrorist financing had actually been detected. There may indeed be an innocent explanation for the activity. The identification of an unusual transaction should however alert the employee to the need to conduct some form of additional procedure, potentially leading to the identification and reporting of an actual suspicion.

The investigation procedures to be adopted are discussed in the next chapter, but these can only follow from alert monitoring, whether conducted by using software solutions or through attentive employee engagement.

To ensure that employees are clear as to what actually represents unusual activity, a clear series of policies needs to be developed, supported by appropriate procedures and systems. Training needs to be implemented which enables employees to appreciate what might be the type of unusual transaction that they would be likely to encounter in the ordinary course of their business. This training needs to be as relevant as possible to the nature of the business that the employee actually undertakes.

THE DEVELOPMENT OF POLICY

The unusual transaction policy will need to be easily understood by all employees, so it needs to be written in a language that they are able to relate to. It will also need to include sufficient information to make it clear to the employee exactly what are the requirements to be complied with. The following is the type of wording that should be considered when developing a short high-level money laundering deterrence policy:

The responsibility for money laundering deterrence resides with Local Compliance or the respective Country AML Officers where applicable, who shall have the responsibility for ensuring that ongoing account and transaction monitoring is conducted to detect unusual or suspicious activities.

As part of our programme of deterring money laundering, each business line is responsible for monitoring all of its customers as well as their financial behaviour. The business lines' management therefore have to be aware of significant transactions and increased activity in the accounts of all of their customers and should implement appropriate systems of identification and reporting. The objective of such systems is to ensure that irregular behaviour (especially unusual or suspicious activities) that is conducted by a customer is recognised immediately by the relevant business line management – and promptly reported to the appropriate person within the business. In order to increase the efficiency of customer monitoring all legal means available to the business unit should be utilised, where possible and appropriate. In case of any doubt the advice of the Group MLRO should be sought.

An unusual or a suspicious activity is defined as a transaction which cannot be explained in any logical way (whether objectively or by the customer). Unusual or suspicious activities may include:

- undertaking account transactions or other activities which are not consistent with the profile of the customer or its group members, or the bank's knowledge of that customer;
- conducting transactions that are above or just below a certain specified threshold amount as set out in our business unit processes and procedures;
- evidence of breaking up amounts before transfer or receipt without a logical explanation or clear business purpose (e.g., 'smurfing') to avoid reporting;
- the regular transference of company funds to private accounts or vice versa;
- the customer requesting or accepting irregular or unusual transaction conditions; and
- the occurrence of any prevailing indicators of unusual or suspicious activities which have been set out by the home or host country authorities in their relevant rules and regulations.

This policy combines the obligations that exist on specific employees, with giving them the information that they may require to enable them to know precisely what this means. We would expect this to be supplemented by a series of real life examples which highlight the specific actions that a particular firm should be required to take. This should be sufficient to enable the employee to judge whether additional investigation is actually required in the circumstances envisaged.

Many firms actually report their responsibilities in this regard in their annual reports. The following is a South African example.

Money laundering control

Legislation across the group pertaining to money laundering and terrorist financing control imposes significant requirements in terms of customer identification, record keeping and training, as well as obligations to detect, prevent and report money laundering and terrorist financing. The group is committed to continually improving its control measures. The group's money laundering and terrorist financing control policy is being amended to accommodate Financial Action Task Force and other best practice requirements.

Global financial crime remains a concern for financial regulators. As a member of the Financial Action Task Force, South Africa underwent a mutual evaluation in 2008 to assess the effectiveness of its money laundering and terrorist financing control framework. The Financial Action Task Force's final report was issued in April 2009 and while there was general approval of the legal enforcement framework, a number of opportunities for improvement were noted. The group attended, upon invitation, the annual Wolfsberg forum in Switzerland. The Wolfsberg Group is an association of eleven global banks that aims to develop financial services industry standards and related products for know your customer, anti-money laundering and counter terrorist financing policies.

Compliance risk management training

Through ongoing training and internal publications, staff are made aware of their responsibilities in terms of legislative and regulatory requirements and developments. These cover topics as diverse as treating customers fairly, money laundering and terrorist financing, market conduct and health and safety requirements, among others.

Source: Standard Bank of South Africa Annual Report 2006

The issues to be addressed here are the same for firms in all countries. No financial institution will wish to be involved directly in assisting money laundering or terrorist financing. The investigation costs that can result from regulatory action, together with the loss of reputation, all serve to raise the importance of the issue of suspicion identification.

THE TYPES OF EVENTS THAT MIGHT CAUSE SUSPICION

There is no definitive list of all of the types of transaction that could represent an unusual transaction. The following is based upon a list prepared for the UK market by the Joint Money Laundering Steering Group but cannot be considered as exhaustive. It does however provide an analysis of matters that should be considered and potentially included within the guidance provided to employees of a financial institution.

The type of things to look out for which may be unusual or could potentially give rise to knowledge or suspicion could include the following:

- Transactions which have no apparent purpose, or which make no obvious economic sense, including where a person makes a loss against tax.
- Transactions which appear to be unnecessarily complex given what is intended.
- The use of nonresident accounts, companies or structures in circumstances where the customer's needs do not appear to support such economic requirements.
- Where the transaction being requested by the customer, or the size or pattern of the transaction, is without reasonable explanation out of the ordinary range of services normally requested or

is inconsistent with the experience of the firm in relation to the particular customer.

- Where the business unit is dealing with customers that would not normally be expected in that part of the business, either due to location or to the nature of the activity conducted.
- Transfers to and from high risk jurisdictions, without reasonable explanation, which are not consistent with the customer's known foreign business dealings or interests.
- Where a series of transactions appears to be structured just below a regulatory threshold with the intention of avoiding internal or regulatory reporting requirements.
- Where a customer who has entered into a business relationship with the firm only uses the relationship for a single transaction, or uses the facilities for only a very short period of time.
- The routing of funds through third party accounts without any obvious legitimate economic purpose.
- The customer undertaking unusual investment transactions without an apparently discernible profitable motive.

Of course it will always be necessary to make these examples relevant to the reader of the policy, aligning the specific risk to the nature of the business activity undertaken. These examples could either be incorporated into the policy manual or the information provided through the medium of a tailored workshop. Without such tailoring the employee will have little understanding of the relevance of the issue to the business that they are undertaking, with the consequence that the necessary monitoring will not be undertaken and the inappropriate activity will not be identified promptly as required.

THE PROBLEMS OF CUSTOMER IDENTIFICATION

Employees must also be vigilant when looking at customer identification, as there are various scenarios, which may highlight unusual behaviour, and possible money laundering activity. The customer identification process may raise specific concerns and the types of things employees should consider will include the following:

- Has the customer refused, or appeared particularly reluctant, to provide the information requested without reasonable explanation?

- Do you understand the legal and corporate structure of the client entity, and its ownership and control, and does the structure appear to make sense?
- Are staff members aware of any inconsistencies between locations and other information provided?
- Is the area of residence given with other profile details, such as employment?
- Does an address appear vague or unusual – e.g., an accommodation agency, a professional registered office or a trading address?
- Does it make sense for the customer to be opening the account or relationship in the jurisdiction he is asking for?
- Is the information that the customer has provided consistent with the banking or other services or facilities that he is seeking?
- Does the supporting documentation add validity to the other information provided by the customer?
- Does the customer have other banking or financial relationships with the firm; does the collected information on all these relationships appear consistent?
- Does the client want to conclude arrangements unusually urgently, against a promise to provide information at a later stage, which is not satisfactorily explained?
- Has the customer suggested changes to a proposed arrangement in order to avoid providing certain information?

Maintaining natural scepticism is key at this stage. The type of customer that is likely to be a money launderer or involved with terrorist financing could easily be one of the best or most profitable customers of the business. They could be using all of the services that the firm provides and not seem particularly concerned about the price. They are also likely to have perfect documents – indeed documents that might be considered as too perfect. So it is not just the unusual that is an issue; the employee needs to have an awareness that there could be problems hidden inside even well documented accounts.

WHAT MIGHT HIGHLIGHT TERRORIST ACTIVITY?

As we have seen, money laundering and terrorist financing are closely connected. Accordingly staff must also be given guidance and examples of activities which suggest potential terrorist financing activity, which might include the following:

- the presence of round sum deposits, followed by the same amount being transferred away as a wire transfer;
- frequent international ATM activity;
- the absence of any known source of income;
- the use of wire transfers and the internet to move funds to and from high risk countries and geographic locations;
- frequent address changes;
- purchases of military items or technology; and
- media reports on suspected, arrested terrorists or groups.

Of course no such list can in itself ever be complete and address all issues. What is needed is for the MLRO or another suitably experienced and independent unit to look closely at the processes and procedures that are maintained by the firm to identify those areas of activity which are most susceptible to inappropriate activity. The attention of employees needs to be directed towards such areas which are inherently therefore more risky for the bank.

Whilst software solutions may enable a firm to identify the transactions that could potentially relate to money laundering or terrorist financing once they have been undertaken, the objective is where possible to avoid the firm undertaking such transactions. Accordingly the first line of defence is the front of house staff of the firm and therefore vigilance and training are always paramount.

Chapter 18

INVESTIGATING SUSPICIONS

THE INVESTIGATION PROCESS

As discussed in the two previous chapters, the first stage of the process of identifying suspicions is the initial identification of a transaction. Following approved company policies the staff member will then need to make a report to an appropriate officer of the firm. Once this initial report has been made to the appropriate officer, the next stage is for an initial investigation to be undertaken by the firm itself. The objective of this stage of the investigation process is to see whether there are actually sufficient suspicions to require this transaction or relationship to be reported to the relevant external reporting body.

There are therefore a number of different parties that will become involved at different stages of the process. Initially it is the responsibility of the firm's own staff and their appointed officer to determine whether there are reasonable grounds for having knowledge or suspicion of inappropriate activity. This means the firm needs to have clearly defined what constitutes an actual suspicion, as well as the procedures that need to be followed internally to ensure that all required internal reporting obligations are also met.

Once internal processes have been completed firms must then submit external reports, generally known as Suspicious Activity Reports (SARs) to the relevant reporting agency. Generally the requirement is that subsequent to such a report having been made, firms must then work with that agency before proceeding further.

The agency may just receive the report and state that no action is to be taken by them, allowing the firm to continue to act normally on the account. However in other cases the reporting agency may either request additional information or require that action be taken on the account, which could include requiring that the customer's funds must be frozen. The legal methods to achieve this do vary between jurisdictions.

MAKING A REPORT

Regulated firms are generally required to make a report to the relevant authorities in respect of information that comes to them in the normal course of business in the regulated sector that is likely to be of interest to the enforcement authorities in their attempts to detect money laundering and the financing of terrorism. This may occur:

- where a firm knows, or
- where a firm suspects, or
- where they have reasonable grounds for knowing or suspecting that a person may be engaged in money laundering or terrorist financing.

Before a suspicious report can be raised there is an obligation on the firm to undertake their own investigations to confirm that there actually is a suspicion as set out in their own internal procedures. Each firm must then ensure that all members of staff report to the firm's nominated officer or MLRO, when they have reasonable grounds for knowledge or suspicion that a person or customer is engaged in money laundering or terrorist financing. It is then for the nominated officer or MLRO to consider the report made by employees of a firm and to consider whether they believe there are actually sufficient grounds for knowledge or suspicion. For such an internal process to work effectively, firms must ensure that staff are adequately trained (Chapter 10) in making reports to nominated officers and MLROs. MLROs must also have received training to enable them adequately to perform their investigating and reporting obligations.

INTERNAL REPORTING

Who should report suspicions?

All relevant employees of a regulated firm are obliged to report to the nominated officer when they have grounds for knowledge or suspicion of money laundering. Therefore, this must be made clear to all employees so that they know who they should report to and the impact on their and the firm's liabilities of failing to do so. Firms may suggest that employees should consult with line managers before sending reports to the nominated officer, but clearly this can only be undertaken if the employee believes that the line manager is not personally involved with the potential inappropriate activity. In such cases there will be additional responsibilities specified concerning the actions that should be taken by the line manager, since this additional stage must not delay the firm in making SAR reports.

The nominated officer is then normally under an obligation to report as soon as is reasonably practical. In this respect, firms must ensure that internal procedures do not prevent or delay reports from reaching nominated officers. They will also need to have procedures agreed with their relevant agencies as to what would constitute an appropriate maximum time for investigation prior to reporting to the relevant agency – indeed it is often delaying such reporting which results in the money launderer succeeding in evading detection. The officer needs to recognise that the piece of information that they are holding may only be part of a much wider story that would only be obvious to the relevant agency, and that delaying provision of information could result in necessary linkages not being made and the criminal avoiding detection.

What should a bank consider when seeking to establish the existence of a reportable suspicion?

It is important to remember that local rules and regulations generally place employees under a legal obligation to decide whether to report a potential suspicion to the nominated officer or not.

Once an employee has made a report to the nominated officer or another officer to whom the nominated officer has delegated responsibility, the employee's statutory obligation would normally have been satisfied and they will be protected by legislation from a regulatory action. In doing this employees should not be unnecessarily influenced by colleagues or allow such a colleague to decide for them whether reporting is appropriate. This is because the colleague could of course be involved in the inappropriate activity, but also because their advice will not change the employee's individual responsibility. The general requirement is that each employee must decide whether to make a report based on the merits of the specific case and their personal knowledge and experience.

Clearly, staff training and awareness of the type of factors to look out for becomes vitally important. In order to ensure maximum efficiency in the reporting process, short reporting lines, with a minimum number of people between the person with the knowledge or suspicion and the nominated officer, are recommended, as they will ensure speed, confidentiality and swift access to the nominated officer.

In terms of the initial investigation by the employee, they need to look dispassionately at the information available to them and then consider whether there could be evidence of either money laundering or an indication of terrorist financing. They need to avoid reporting just because they "do not like the look of someone" and ensure that there is really some evidence. Some people may appear to be "shifty" or "creepy", but this does not mean that they are actually criminal. Comments like this do not have any place in the investigation documentation and could prejudice later actions since this presupposes inappropriate conduct using a judgement formed on an inappropriate basis.

The employee should promptly obtain all of the information available to them and make their initial judgement based on the facts that then present themselves. Of course, if there is any doubt, then they should report.

How should reports be made?

It is clearly important that reports of suspicions made to the nominated officer are appropriately documented, with a combination of physical and electronic recording normally being required. What needs to be included in a report made by an employee to a reporting officer is normally specified in the relevant firm's rules and regulations. The MLRO would want such reports to include full details of the transaction or relationship which gives rise to the knowledge or suspicion together with details of the customer who is the subject of the report. Without this information the MLRO would be unable to identify whether a suspicion actually exists and therefore they would only then be required to request such information from the relevant employee.

All internal enquiries subsequently made by the MLRO should also be documented. The documentation produced by the MLRO and maintained by the firm meets a number of objectives. Firstly it enables the MLRO to provide additional information to the relevant authorities in case of additional requests for information being made. Secondly it also provides evidence that the MLRO has followed best practice and undertaken the work that the regulations require leading to the suspicion being confirmed or disapproved. In this way the MLRO is also protected in being able to produce evidence that they have been diligent in conducting their investigations.

It is also best practice for all subsequent transactions or activity concerning a customer that is the subject of a report to be reported to the MLRO as they arise, until a report is received from the responsible agency that the customer is no longer under any form of suspicion. It will be for the MLRO to judge whether additional information should be passed on to the relevant authorities and this will often be based on communications that pass between the MLRO and the agency concerned.

EXTERNAL REFERRALS

Once an internal report has been made by a firm, which the MLRO or nominated officer believes to give rise to grounds for knowledge or suspicion, they must report the matter to the relevant agency set up locally to receive such reports, for example the Serious Organised Crime Agency in the UK.

As we have discussed, a referral from the nominated officer or MLRO of suspicious activity must be made as soon as it is practical, if the officer has sufficient grounds for suspicion. One of the many problems in this area is that the actual rules implemented locally may not be very clear as to the actual obligations that are placed on the MLRO in terms of either investigating or the timetable for reporting. In practice, it may actually be difficult to know at which point it is reasonably practical to report to the relevant agency, particularly where it seems the time frame has been left as ambiguously defined. What is clear is that the MLRO does not need to have found out everything prior to making a report. The key issue is this: at what point have they really become suspicious? Once they are – then they should report. They can always send additional information later and indeed many regulators have specifically defined an additional information reporting process for precisely this purpose.

Generally a prompt transferral to the relevant agency is required once an internal report has been made. Employees need to be aware that once a report has been referred, they are then under an obligation not to inform the customer that a report has been made, hence the offence of tipping off (see Chapter 20). Indeed they should avoid discussing the case with anyone to the maximum extent possible, including colleagues.

WHAT IS MEANT BY "KNOWLEDGE" AND "SUSPICION"?

These two concepts are clearly of paramount importance, yet their actual meaning can be unclear. Neither is a precise term and both can be subject to different interpretations. Generally having knowledge means actually knowing something to be true. An individual must actually know that a person was engaged in money laundering or terrorist financing activity. It is recognised that knowledge can also be inferred from surrounding circumstances. It can also be inferred from a scenario where the existence of money laundering should have been obvious to any reasonable and adequately trained employee. However normally there is a recognition that knowledge must only come to the firm in the course of business or as a consequence of making a relevant disclosure to the appropriate agency. If information comes to a firm in any other way it must be disregarded and employees will not be under an obligation to submit a report.

This in practice means that information received as a newspaper report, through electronic media or even as an unsubstantiated phone call must be disregarded as far as is possible. We would emphasise that blogs and reports on the internet are by nature extremely unreliable and should not be used, including ones from so-called reputable electronic sources. There may be little substantive evidence to support the claims made.

The term suspicion is even more subjective and must be proven by the firm who must produce evidence that there really is a suspicion if this is required by the relevant authority. This is to ensure that the reporting agency is not swamped by a high level of unnecessary and unhelpful information. Suspicion is typically defined by the courts as being something which has a foundation but which is beyond mere speculation. So suspicion is not about guesswork, rather there does need to be something concrete to support the concerns.

It is also worth mentioning that an unusual transaction will not necessarily be a suspicious transaction. Customers may have perfectly rational reasons to explain unusual patterns of transactions or account activity. The existence of an unusual pattern should initiate further investigation within the firm, but will not alone result in outright suspicion. It is important to document the investigation of suspicious patterns, since they may later support a suspicion and an obligation to report will then arise. However if an appropriate explanation is received to suggest that the unusual pattern is in fact normal activity, then no additional suspicion exists – although the explanation should still be recorded. This again protects both the firm and its officers by demonstrating that they have acted in accordance with best practice.

WHAT IS MEANT BY "REASONABLE GROUNDS" TO KNOW OR SUSPECT?

As we have seen, employees are under an obligation to report to a nominated officer when they have suspicions or actual knowledge of money laundering/terrorist financing. Failure to do this can generally result in a criminal offence having being committed by the employee. Therefore it is essential for the bank to know when reasonable grounds exist for knowing or suspecting that a person is engaged in money laundering and/or terrorist financing.

Generally firms develop an objective test of suspicion based on guidance provided to them by their relevant authority. The test will be met when it can be demonstrated by a known member of staff that facts or circumstances exist from which a reasonable person engaged in a business subject to money laundering regulations would have inferred knowledge, or formed the suspicion that another person was engaged in money laundering or terrorist financing.

The test will always operate on the balance of probability. Put at its simplest any transaction could be money laundering or terrorist financing, but most are not. Consequently the information required and its assessment will vary on a case-by-case basis. Problems particularly occur in cases of complex transactions and unusual circumstances where it will prove to be particularly difficult to establish that there really is evidence of a suspicion.

Unless it is particularly obvious, employees will not always be able to spot when reasonable grounds to know or suspect money laundering will exist. However employees must be able to defend themselves against a charge that they failed to meet the objective test for suspicion. They can do this by demonstrating that they took reasonable steps in the particular circumstances, in the context of a risk-based approach, to know the customer and the rationale for the transaction, activity or instruction. Therefore, effective customer due diligence becomes vitally important.

THE INVESTIGATION BY THE NOMINATED OFFICER

After reporting to the nominated officer, they will need to conduct a higher level of investigation leading to an assessment of the suspicion and if necessary the preparation and issuance of a money laundering report.

The first obligation for the firm's nominated officer is that they must receive and consider all reports forwarded to them by employees. It is then for the nominated officer to determine whether the reports give rise to knowledge or suspicion, or reasonable grounds for suspicion. In order for the nominated officer to effectively carry out this role they must have access to any information that they consider necessary to enable them to conduct their role, particularly the firm's know your customer information.

The nominated officer may also wish to gain further information from an intermediary who may have introduced the customer to the firm or, if necessary, obtain information directly from the customer. Obtaining information from the customer must only be considered in exceptional circumstances as such an approach may alert the customer that money laundering deterrence disclosure is being considered. The nominated advisor may find it easier for a customer facing employee to obtain such information, as the nominated officer by their very role is likely to alert customers, and is also more at risk of tipping off the customer.

There are a number of factors which a nominated officer must address when considering an internal suspicion report. There will inevitably be a balance to be struck between the risk posed by the transaction or activity being addressed and the time it may take to make a relevant disclosure to the appropriate authorities. Time delays are likely to occur as consent is sought and searches are made of unlinked systems and records that might hold relevant information.

An extensive review may entail looking at known connected accounts or relationships which will need to be examined. Considering the time constraints involved when reporting, nominated officers may wish to make an initial report prior to completing a full review of linked and connected relationships. It may be worthwhile to document this stage as much as possible, as any delays in reporting suspicions may be interpreted as the suspicion not being reported "as soon as is reasonably practical". This will be particularly important in the event that the nominated officer decides not to make a full report. In such a scenario the nominated officer should keep all activity clearly documented, or recorded electronically and retained with the internal suspicion report.

REPORTING IN THE UK

The UK rules on reporting are typical of those adopted elsewhere and can be considered to represent international best practice in this regard.

Reporting to the Serious Organised Crime Agency (SOCA)

In the UK the nominated officer must report to SOCA any transaction or activity which they reasonably suspect may be linked to money laundering. A Suspicious Activity Report (or SAR) must be submitted as soon as is reasonably practical after the information becomes available.

Firms should include in each SAR as much relevant information about the customer, transaction or activity as it has in its records. In particular law enforcement agencies have indicated that details of an individual's occupation/company's business and National Insurance number are valuable in enabling them to access other relevant information about the customer. As there is no obligation to collect this information, a firm may not hold these details for all its customers. However, where it has obtained this information it would be helpful to include it as part of a SAR made by a firm.

When is there no obligation to report?

In circumstances where neither the identity of the fraudster, nor the location of the criminal property is known or likely to be discovered, there will generally not be an obligation to report since there is limited usable information available for disclosure. For example, when a person loses a cheque book or debit card, this can lead to multiple low value fraudulent transactions over a period of time of relatively little importance to the reporting agency.

Generally speaking, there will be no obligation to make a report, where none of the following are known or suspected:

- the identity of the person who is engaged in money laundering;
- the whereabouts of any of the laundered property;
- any of the information that is available would assist in identifying that person, or the whereabouts of the laundered property.

SANCTIONS AND PENALTIES FOR FAILING TO COMPLY

The regulations in each country will specify the sanctions or penalties for failing to comply with a reporting regime.

Normally where a person fails to make disclosures to a nominated officer and/or the nominated officer fails to make a report to the relevant agency as soon as is practical, firms, employees and nominated officers as appropriate will be subject to criminal prosecution or regulatory censure. In the UK a criminal prosecution can result in the penalty of imprisonment for up to five years and/or a fine.

Chapter 19

ONGOING MONITORING

THE IMPORTANCE OF ONGOING MONITORING

In Chapter 11 we discussed the know your customer obligations which are one of the main money laundering deterrence measures that are available to a firm. Such due diligence enables a firm to really understand their clients and therefore to potentially identify that they are undertaking inappropriate activity.

Undertaking primary investigation into the business intentions and credibility of a customer is fundamental when distinguishing a legitimate business interest from a business that is in fact a facade used for furthering criminal intentions. However initial identification work is only the starting point in the money laundering and terrorist financing monitoring process that a firm will implement. The initial due diligence conducted needs to be supplemented by appropriate and sensible ongoing continuous customer and transaction monitoring.

Any money launderer or terrorist financer will obviously have expected customer due diligence to have been carried out by a firm. Accordingly they would have found documents and solutions in order to comply with the firm's systems and controls and avoid creating suspicion at this stage. This would ensure that they would get past the initial stage of placing illegal proceeds into a legitimate source. It is during the later layering and integration stages that the firm probably has the best opportunity to identify inappropriate activity.

If we consider a business case, a money launderer will often register what appears to be a legitimate business and will then initially conduct activity that is consistent with the firm's expectations. At this stage the firm will not consider that the account is operating inappropriately and no likelihood of reporting or suspicion would take place. Subsequently the money launderer will start to introduce illicit funds into the account, using small amounts at first and large amounts later. It is at this point where analysis of the behaviour of the customer is necessary. What the firm is seeking to identify is customer activity that appears inconsistent with the firm's understanding of the customer and the nature of business being conducted.

If such activity is closely monitored it is possible for a firm to highlight unusual patterns of activity, which can alert the firm to the possibility of the account being used for money laundering. Clearly initial due diligence cannot adequately predict how a customer relationship will develop. Therefore, ongoing monitoring is required to supplement the initial due diligence and alert the firm to any suspicious circumstances or activity which may later arise.

THE LINK TO CUSTOMER RELATIONSHIP MANAGEMENT

So the objective of ongoing monitoring of the business relationship is to help identify unusual activity. There is a clear link to customer relationship management which needs to be explored. Customer relationship management has the objective of considering a customer relationship and identifying that a specific type and nature of customer should acquire certain products. It is of benefit to a firm in highlighting potential sales to existing customers since it says that a customer of this nature would normally be expected to acquire the following products.

Clearly the ongoing money laundering deterrence monitoring obligation is really just the inverse of this. It takes the normal nature of customer relationships, potentially parameterised, and identifies transactions which are unusual for this type of customer. What this means is that software solutions and approaches that are used for customer relationship management may potentially be used in their inverse to identify unusual patterns of customer activity that may represent inappropriate activity.

An effective monitoring system should flag up transactions and activities for further examination, based on a probabilistic assessment of the nature of the activity conducted. These reports should be reviewed promptly by the appropriate person, and necessary action must be taken in response to the findings, or further examination undertaken.

WHAT DOES ONGOING MONITORING INVOLVE?

There is no single way in which such monitoring should be conducted and approaches vary considerably. The ongoing monitoring will typically include:

- scrutiny of transactions undertaken throughout the course of the relationship (including where necessary the source of funds), to ensure that the transactions are consistent with the firm's knowledge of the customer, their business and risk profile;
- ensuring that the documents, data or information held by the firm are kept up to date.

Customer transactions should be monitored over different periods of time to identify trends within the activity. This needs to be both across the business cycle and within cycles. Where possible it would be advantageous for transactions to be monitored in real time, where transactions are reviewed as they take place or are about to take place.

ENHANCED ONGOING MONITORING

Certain customer relationships and transactions will require ongoing monitoring as a result of their very nature. Circumstances which may attract such enhanced ongoing monitoring will typically include:

- **Specific types of transactions** This can include high risk transactions, however defined. These could include transactions that involve transfers of large amounts of funds, such as the acquisition or disposal of commercial property.

- **The profile of the customer** A customer may by their nature represent a particularly high risk in light of their personal background, for example, customers who are PEPs or businesses that have a large volume of cash transactions, for example casinos.

- **The parties concerned** If a payment has been made to a person or business which appears on a sanctions list then this would clearly make the payee account high risk.

- **Comparison of the activity of the customer with the profile of a similar customer** Accounts of certain businesses may show income which is higher than is normally expected from a business in the same industry sector. A comparison of the level of profits made by a similar business in the same industry sector or trade may raise awareness to the possibility of money laundering.

- **Unusual transactions** A transaction may appear as abnormal due to its very nature. It might be an abnormal size, for example larger than transactions that are normally conducted. On the other hand it might be a transaction which is unusual by its nature in that transactions of such a type are not normally conducted, or are not normally conducted by this type of business. There can also be transactions that are unusual due to their frequency.

- **The nature of a series of transactions** The types of things that tend to give concern here include large volumes of credit notes or adjustments. It is often only when a series of transactions is looked at in the collective that the unusual pattern of behaviour can be identified.

- **Geographic area** The destination or origin of payments may be in a high risk country, such as one appearing towards the lower reaches of the Transparency International list, as shown in the Annex. Such countries may well be considered as representing an increased risk of inappropriate activity and therefore accounts involved with these countries will require a higher level of ongoing monitoring.

- **Product risk** Some products may represent higher than normal risk for an institution and therefore require enhanced monitoring. There is no prescriptive list of such products, but cash collection accounts and complex savings products could, for example, fall into this category.

It is always for the firm to identify what would be considered as high risk in their specific circumstances. A type of business that would be considered as normal for one type of bank could, for example, appear as completely abnormal for another. If you consider an institution that works in a local area providing finance for property and taking deposits, then an overseas corporate account might appear as unusual and therefore high risk. For an internationally active bank such activity would be considered as routine. Therefore each firm needs to undertake some form of risk assessment to develop the criteria to be used to define what might be considered as unusual and then to implement such systems and controls as are necessary to ensure that such transactions are promptly identified and reviewed.

Another area of higher risk is where there is no regular face-to-face contact with customers. This can often be the position with firms that provide credit cards through some form of distance selling process – the internet for example. If regular contact is expected, but does not occur, then this also could be a warning that the customer relationship represents a higher than expected risk.

THE RISK OF DORMANT ACCOUNTS

One area that represents a particularly high risk is that of dormant accounts. In these cases the concern is that the account may be abused by employees of the firm, with funds being diverted for personal use in some way.

Any movement in a dormant account is likely to be a concern and the maintenance of background information on dormant accounts may also prove useful. A clear definition of what might be considered as being dormant needs to have been implemented consistently by the firm. This should include looking for any form of approach that could be used by an employee to prevent an account from being classed as dormant.

A typical case involved an ex-policeman who was jailed in November 2009 over a £1.43 m fraud. The former constable, Stephen Spellacy, was a cocaine addict who had served with Humberside police for 13 years. He was assisted by John Taylor who had worked with Norwich Union (now Aviva) for 12 years before he took advantage of his position. The fraud lasted for several years with Norwich Union dormant accounts being accessed and the cash extracted – and subsequently laundered. The important issue about dormant accounts is that the owners of the accounts cannot be traced, so they are unlikely to complain when the funds are removed. The pair were identified when a £1.1m transfer made by Taylor was investigated, although the fraud had operated without identification due to the large amount of cash that was generally transferred daily by Norwich Union.

This type of event highlights the problem in that it is the staff of the firm that has the best idea as to how to take advantage of the systems that exist and therefore to exploit loopholes. Accordingly enhanced due diligence on staff activity and accounts may well also be appropriate.

Since there is no customer activity on a dormant account, the reliance that can normally be placed upon the customer monitoring their account cannot take place. The same type of risk can exist for any account where the customer is distant from the bank or reliant upon a bank employee for the receipt of customer information.

Therefore dormant and similar distant accounts which are recognised as being high risk, as well as customers who are considered high risk, may require enhanced monitoring, to effectively deal with the high risk nature of the business relationship.

WHAT TYPE OF ENHANCED MONITORING IS REQUIRED?

Monitoring customers and transactions need not necessarily be a complex and sophisticated process. The scope and complexity of a monitoring system must be determined by taking into account the firm's business activities and the size of the firm. While monitoring of transactions and customer activity can be done using either manual or automated systems, the use of software significantly assists the process.

Key elements of any monitoring system should include having up-to-date customer information, which will afford the opportunity to spot the unusual, and ask pertinent questions to elicit an explanation or the reason for unusual transactions or activities. The aim for such a process is to be able to judge circumstances which may appear suspicious leading to further investigation being conducted to identify or disprove a suspicion.

AUTOMATED VS. MANUAL SYSTEMS OF MONITORING

A review of a transaction database by an employee can result in a manual report of transactions that need to be investigated, but it is very hard from such a cursory review to identify unusual trends in individual accounts. Similarly reports may also be generated based on analytical software applications on a standard periodic basis. The chosen system of monitoring will depend on the size and nature of the firm, as a firm which has major issues of volume may need to implement a more sophisticated automated system which is programmed to pick up certain factors which appear to make a transaction suspicious.

The automated transaction monitoring systems available on the market use a variety of techniques to detect and report unusual/uncharacteristic activity. The techniques used range from artificial intelligence to simple rules. The nature of the systems available is further described in Chapter 23. Further investigation and analyses from the output from such systems may lead to a valid suspicion of money laundering. However, such systems may be difficult to implement and maintain due to their reliance on customer reference and transaction data.

There is a danger when using an automated system that customers and transactions are not monitored on a personalised basis, but on a standard characterised basis. Consequently some form of continued personal review to supplement such monitoring is still preferable.

ISSUES TO CONSIDER WHEN IMPLEMENTING A MONITORING SYSTEM

Automated and manual systems vary in the approach they take to monitoring customer transactions as discussed above. Firms must essentially evaluate their own objectives, in terms of what they wish to achieve from their monitoring system in order to assess which systems best suit their business needs. The kind of questions which firms should address when selecting a monitoring system which meets their needs include the following:

- How does the solution enable the firm to implement a risk-based approach to assessing the risk inherent in transactions conducted with customers and third parties?
- How do the system's parameters assist with the risk-based approach and lead to a reasonable correlation between transaction alerts and the incidence of money laundering or terrorist financing?
- What are the levels of investigation that the firm is capable of undertaking and will the system produce a high level of false positives which impact the delivery of an effective programme of monitoring?
- What are the different types of money laundering and terrorist financing that are addressed by the system and are these consistent with the activities conducted by the firm?
- What are the data requirements of the system and has the firm recorded the data necessary to support the required analysis?

STAFF TRAINING

Apart from a computerised monitoring system which produces reports, firms should also recognise the importance of staff awareness as discussed in Chapter 10. Providing adequate training to staff is a direct and cost-effective method of continuously monitoring customers and transactions.

The importance of employees' experience and intuition should not be ignored. Such knowledge can add considerably to a firm's ability to meet its ongoing monitoring obligations as a result of the following factors:

- Staff intuition is important as employees with experience are able to spot suspicious activity through their personal knowledge of the nature of the customer, identifying patterns and concerns which would go undetected with a computerised reporting method.
- Customer facing employees benefit from direct exposure to a customer face-to-face, so they are able to witness changes in the customer's physical behaviour which could give rise to suspicion.
- Customer facing employees also benefit from telephone conversations with customers, and will be able to analyse the tone of voice and language used by customers which could potentially arouse suspicion.
- They also have practical experience of dealing with previous customers with similar backgrounds, which enables such employees to recognise differences which may give rise to suspicion.

Chapter 20

TIPPING OFF

INTRODUCTION

It is easy to focus almost entirely on the steps taken to identify and investigate criminal activity when seeking to combat money laundering. However, attention must also be given to the direction of the employees and those who work internally within a firm. Money laundering deterrence is also dependent on the discretion of those who investigate and report suspicions of money laundering. The prevention of money laundering would be severely undermined if money launderers were alerted as soon as a suspicion arose since the funds would most likely disappear to another jurisdiction.

LETTING THE CUSTOMER KNOW

Letting the money launderer find out that they are under suspicion is generally referred to as tipping off. Generally once an internal or external suspicion report has been made it is a criminal offence for anyone to release information which is likely to prejudice an investigation. Persons entrusted with investigating and reporting duties must essentially conduct customer enquiries in a tactful manner regarding the background to a transaction or activity that is inconsistent with the normal pattern of activity, and carry out enhanced customer due diligence measures in a way which does not give rise to the customer being aware that they are under suspicion.

Typically the offence of tipping off is defined as follows. A person commits an offence if:

(a) he knows or suspects that a disclosure has been made, and
(b) he makes a disclosure which is likely to prejudice any investigation which might be conducted following the disclosure referred to above.

A person does not normally commit an offence if he did not know or suspect that the disclosure was likely to be prejudicial. Perhaps the real issue to consider here is what a reasonable person might judge that the employee did know or suspect, since in a court hearing there is always the risk that a measure of hindsight might be taken into account.

It is normally an offence for a person to make a disclosure to a customer or associate that was likely to prejudice any investigation that might be brought following the making of a suspicious activity report (SAR) to the relevant reporting agency, when that person knew or suspected that a SAR had been made. An offence would not be committed unless a SAR had been filed since in the absence of reporting there is no actual suspicion.

What this means is that all members of staff at a financial institution need to be fully aware of their obligations under tipping off legislation. They need to know what to say to a customer and what to do to avoid alerting them to the concerns that they may actually be harbouring. This needs training and role playing to appreciate the issues that may arise in practice.

THE PROBLEMS IN PRACTICE

One of the concerns is what an employee should actually do when they need to identify a potential case of money laundering or terrorist financing. Naturally they will wish to obtain further information and to undertake enhanced due diligence, but they need to do this in such a way as to ensure that the customer does not become unduly suspicious. Often they will fall back on standard comments such as "our standard procedures require me to ask the following question" or "this is one of the general compliance things we have to deal with". By attempting to make the due diligence processes appear as a standard process, the employee will attempt to obtain relevant information without unnecessarily alerting the customer. An employee should never say: "we are doing this as part of our money laundering deterrence checks", since this could take the conversation along a line that might be uncomfortable.

If a customer is undertaking inappropriate activity it is often junior staff that are the first to speak to the customer. Even moving responsibility unusually up the line of command could alert the customer to concerns and potentially be considered as tipping off. Therefore front line staff need to be extremely vigilant in what they do and be fully aware of the processes and procedures that are to be undertaken. They may be provided with a script which they should follow in such cases, although showing the script to the customer would also clearly be tipping off.

To illustrate how difficult matters can get, consider the following example. If a bank manager learns from the bank's MLRO that the relevant regulatory body is contemplating making an investigation into a customer's transactions and no report has yet been made by the firm, the bank manager will normally commit an offence if they disclose the fact that a report is even being contemplated in light of the customer's transactions. In such a case a SAR will not have been issued, yet the bank manager is still at risk.

PENALTIES FOR TIPPING OFF

There are normally major penalties for tipping off since this could prevent the criminal funds being seized. If the customer is tipped off then they will continue to launder their funds through another medium and typically from another place. Five years' imprisonment and unlimited fines are quite normal penalties to have imposed for tipping off, so all employees do need to take their responsibilities seriously.

COMMUNICATIONS WITH CUSTOMERS UNDER INVESTIGATION

Once a suspicion has been notified through the submission of a SAR to the relevant agency, the condition of the tipping off offence continues. Firms cannot tell the customer the real reason why their transaction is being delayed, as informing the customer that a report is awaiting consent from the relevant agency would obviously give rise to the offence of tipping off. The issue is clear. If the bank has received instructions from their relevant authority to freeze an account then they cannot tell the customer why the account is frozen. As you would expect, they will run out of excuses relatively quickly and the customer will become suspicious. For how long can you blame the bank's IT systems for failing to process a transaction or transfer? While the customer may at that stage disappear, at least the frozen funds will be available for the enforcement officers to investigate.

The harder case is where a report has been made but there has been no response from the relevant agency. Normally if the bank or financial institution is acting in good faith and failing to conduct a transaction would have the effect of tipping off the customer, then regulation will normally specifiy that the firm should undertake the transaction, even though the effect of this may be moving the funds to another jurisdiction.

In all cases the MLRO should be involved to ensure that the actions taken by the bank or financial institution are in accordance with the regulations applying in the relevant jurisdiction.

Chapter 21

RECORD KEEPING

THE PURPOSE OF RECORD KEEPING

Record keeping is an essential feature of money laundering legislation in most countries. There is generally an obligation on firms to maintain appropriate money laundering deterrence records and controls in relation to the firm's business, with the idea being that maintaining an adequate audit trail is an essential component of combating money laundering. Typically there will be a requirement to retain records concerning customer identification and transactions as evidence of work they have undertaken in complying with their legal and regulatory obligations. Such information may also be used as evidence in the event that an investigation is conducted by law enforcement. Not only must records exist, but generally firms must take reasonable care to keep adequate records appropriate to the scale, nature and complexity of the business.

WHAT RECORDS HAVE TO BE KEPT?

The exact details of which records must be kept will vary between jurisdictions. The general objective of such rules is to ensure that the firm is able to provide details of the audit trail in the event that the firm's customer is investigated. The type of records maintained usually includes the following:

- Customer information
- Transactions
- Internal and external suspicion reports
- Investigation records
- MLRO annual reports
- Information not acted on
- Actions taken resulting from agency requests
- Training and compliance monitoring
- Information about the effectiveness of training.

Customer identification

You would expect the firm to keep a copy of references and other evidence of a customer's identity, which has been obtained during the process of customer due diligence. Copies of identification certificates should also generally be kept. Additional information which has been obtained as a result of enhanced due diligence should also be maintained for the purposes of ongoing monitoring.

Where a financial institution is not able to produce the necessary evidence of identity, they will generally be required to provide enough evidence to enable the document to be reobtained from the source of issue. The information needed in order to do this will normally include information on the type of document, its number, date and place of issue. There will be requirements as to the period for which customer identification information must be kept, with a period of up to five years after the relationship with the customer has ended being frequently used. The end of the relationship is, in the case of an occasional transaction, the date which is the last in a series of transactions. In the case of a longer term business relationship ending, the termination date is the date when the account was closed.

Transactions

Regulations normally require that transactions which are carried out throughout the duration of the business relationship be kept as part of the firm's records. Records of transactions can be in numerous forms such as credit and debit slips, cheques and correspondence. Firms need to ensure that they are maintained in a form where a satisfactory audit trail may be compiled and a financial profile established for any suspect account or customer.

Again the length of time for which such records will need to be maintained will be specified in local regulations, with a period of up to five years from the date on which the transaction is completed being quite normal. However if the transaction relates to an asset where a claim against the firm could exist for a period in excess of five years then it may well be appropriate for the firm to implement a longer retention period than that which is specifically required by money laundering deterrence regulations to adequately protect the firm.

Internal and external reports

It is normally a requirement that firms must make and retain records of all actions taken under the internal and external reporting requirements. As part of this, firms should also keep records of when the nominated officer (or MLRO) has considered information or other material concerning possible money laundering, but has not made a report to the relevant authority. Obviously copies of any suspicious activity reports actually made should also be retained.

Again local regulations will specify the retention period, but generally all external and internal reports should be retained for a period of up to five years from the date when the report was made.

It may also prove useful to a firm to retain records of the following:

- procedures undertaken prior to hiring staff to ensure that they are fit and proper;
- details of staff that have received anti-money laundering induction training on joining the firm;
- dates of when anti-money laundering training was given;
- the nature of the training;
- the names of staff who received the training;
- the results of any tests undertaken by staff to show that they really understood the training;
- reports made by the MLRO to senior management;
- records of consideration of those reports and of any action taken as a consequence;
- internal audit reports relating to money laundering deterrence policies, processes and procedures.

IN WHAT FORM SHOULD RECORDS BE KEPT?

Firms will retain reports with a view to reducing the volume and density of records, whilst still complying with statutory records retention rules. The extent to which this is permitted within a particular jurisdiction will vary, with some jurisdictions requiring that only and all original documents should be retained. The following are the options that may be considered in terms of recoding information:

- by way of original documentation;
- by way of photocopies of original documents;
- on microfiche;
- in scanned form;
- in computerised or electronic form.

It is important to recognise that the record retention periods and rules are normally unaffected by the format in which the records are kept. Aside from money laundering obligations, records should be accessible and readily retrievable when rationalising computer systems and physical storage arrangements for firms involved in mergers and takeovers. There are generally no locations specified by regulations as to where records should be kept, simply a requirement that they should be retrievable without undue delay.

Firms have a responsibility to ensure that records held outside their country also meet the same record-keeping requirements. No secrecy or data protection legislation should be allowed to restrict access to records either by the firm and its officers, or by the home country law enforcement agencies under court order or relevant mutual assistance procedures. If such restrictions do exist, copies of the underlying records of identity should be sought where possible, and retained in the home country. Firms which operate internationally will need to take into account the anti-money laundering and counter-terrorist financing legislation in all countries in which they operate and to make sure that the record-keeping requirements of such countries are compatible with home country legislation.

Once records have been requested by relevant law enforcement agencies and are being used as part of ongoing investigations, the records should be retained until the firm is informed by the relevant authority that the case has been closed. However, if a firm has not been advised of an ongoing investigation within five years of a disclosure having been made, the records may generally be destroyed in compliance with the normal record-keeping procedure, although the rules of the local jurisdiction could vary this requirement. When a firm is deciding upon its retentions policy, financial sector businesses must weigh the statutory requirements with the needs of the investigating authorities in the light of normal commercial considerations.

FAILURE TO KEEP RECORDS

If a firm fails to comply with the record-keeping obligations then the firm or the individual involved can be subject to prosecution, which can include imprisonment for up to year and/or a fine, or regulatory censure. Consequently record keeping does need to be taken seriously by both the firm and its appointed officers.

Chapter 22

RISK MANAGEMENT

THE RELATIONSHIP BETWEEN MONEY LAUNDERING DETERRENCE AND TERRORIST FINANCING PROGRAMMES AND RISK MANAGEMENT

Within a financial institution there is a general requirement to implement an effective enterprise risk management programme which captures each risk once. As such the risk of a firm being involved with either money laundering deterrence or terrorist financing will fall within this general structure of risk management.

This is a risk that is within the remit of the firm's operational risk management programme, with the risk management team facilitating the implementation of adequate control, monitoring and reporting procedures within the business.

The chief risk officer will rely upon the work conducted by the MLRO to ensure that the business has adequately mitigated this risk, providing the MLRO with the necessary risk ownership, but monitoring that such work is efficiently and effectively conducted.

The MLRO is one of the risk soldiers on whom the chief risk officer relies, along with compliance officers and internal auditors, to ensure that the necessary independent monitoring of risk is conducted. Therefore the work that is undertaken by the MLRO will be built into the risk management framework required by the firm and monitored by the Risk Committee.

THE RISK OF MONEY LAUNDERING AND TERRORIST FINANCING

The inherent risk involved with money laundering deterrence and terrorist financing, that is the risk of loss without controls, is generally high. If a firm fails to implement effective money laundering systems and controls then this is likely to come to the attention of money launderers and terrorist financiers who will generally exploit any perceived weaknesses in the control environment.

The MLRO and business managers implement a series of controls, systems and processes to mitigate such risks, resulting in what is called residual risk. This is the risk of loss that results from the implementation of the control environment as demonstrated by the losses and events that actually occur in practice.

For a loss to be incurred a firm needs to be thought of as being involved with either a money launderer or someone engaged in terrorist financing. There is no requirement for any actual involvement to take place in order for a loss to occur in terms of reputation. Reputational loss will be incurred purely from the publication of the allegation regardless of whether it is in fact correct. Of course if the allegation is proven a series of additional losses could be incurred by the firm, including penalties from a regulator.

The loss of reputation is perhaps the greatest risk. Normal personal or corporate customers are likely to be concerned at being involved with a firm that has been found guilty of harbouring money launderers or being engaged in terrorist financing. Consequently a loss of customer confidence and business is likely to occur.

Secondly there are the costs of the investigation that will be required if a true case of money laundering or terrorist financing occurs. This should not be underestimated and could involve a detailed review of documentation and patterns of behaviour, potentially across a range of jurisdictions. This tends to put major pressure on appointed officers and other relevant staff with potentially adverse consequences.

Thirdly the regulator may impose a requirement on the firm to retrain all staff to ensure that in future they are aware of their obligations, or even to repeat identification procedures on all customers. Any such activity will of course prove to be expensive both in terms of cost and also management time.

Finally there is the risk of penalties from the regulator. Such a case occurred at Abbey National (now Banco Santander), a retail bank in the UK which was reported by the Financial Services Authority (FSA) in December 2003.

In this case, prior to November 2000 Abbey National had a system of centralised monitoring of compliance with its anti-money laundering ("AML") policies and procedures. However, from November 2000, due to a reallocation of resources, the approach was amended so that reliance was placed on a branch self-certification process. The management information that was produced by this self-certification process was not sufficient for the central MLRO function adequately to assess Abbey National's compliance with money laundering deterrence regulations.

In March 2003 Abbey National's Group Internal Audit function carried out a review of Abbey National's compliance with its customer identification requirements. The report identified substantial failures in the adherence to the requirements, including non compliance rates of 32% in respect of the identification of new customers.

In addition to the substantial failures reported by the auditors, the investigators identified serious failures in relation to Suspicious Activity Reports (SARs). Of the SARs that Abbey National submitted to the National Criminal Intelligence Service (NCIS) [now the Serious Organised Crime Agency, or SOCA] in respect of transactions occurring during 2002, over half were submitted more than 30 days after they had been reported internally to the central MLRO function, with the last one not submitted until October 2003.

In so doing the FSA judged that Abbey National demonstrated extremely serious failings that demanded a very substantial financial penalty. These failings were viewed by the FSA as being particularly serious in light of the following factors:

1. In respect of transactions undertaken or attempted by customers in 2002, the failure to ensure that suspicious transactions were considered and reported promptly to NCIS by Abbey National's central MLRO function demonstrated that, in the past, Abbey National had shown such a marked lack of regard for its regulatory obligations as to present a substantial risk to the FSA's statutory objectives, including the reduction of financial crime.
2. The failure by Abbey National adequately to monitor compliance with money laundering also demonstrated that, in the past, Abbey National had shown such a marked lack of regard for its regulatory obligations as again to present a substantial risk to the FSA's statutory objectives.
3. A failure rate of 32% in the identification of customers is of itself very serious.

The FSA stated that it is a cornerstone of the UK's AML regime that regulated firms must report promptly information about suspicious transactions that their customers have entered into or are attempting to enter into. An essential element of the reporting requirement is that firms obtain and keep sufficient evidence of their customers' identity to enable law enforcement to identify individuals involved in money laundering and to link them with criminal funds attempting to pass through the UK financial system. This is absolutely vital in assisting the detection, investigation and prevention of financial crime.

In failing to ensure that suspicious transactions were reported on a timely basis and to identify their customers properly, the FSA took the view that Abbey National had potentially hindered the ability of law enforcement to detect and prosecute money launderers. Furthermore, its failure to monitor compliance adequately had left it open to abuse by money launderers and consequent reputational risk.

The FSA considered that Abbey's failings were indicative of wider systems and control failings across the Abbey National Group over a prolonged period of time. The wider failings included inadequate monitoring of key regulatory risks and inadequate identification and gathering of key management information. The overall control environment and, in particular, overall compliance monitoring was viewed as having been weak across the Group.

The FSA stated that without the effective remedial steps taken by Abbey National after April 2003, the penalty would have been substantially greater. In view of all the circumstances the FSA decided to impose a financial penalty of £2 000 000.

The risks are clear to see. A publicised penalty of such magnitude would have a significant impact on the reputation of the firm and its ability to operate successfully. On 26 July 2004 the board of Abbey National agreed to a takeover from Banco Santander of Spain.

MONEY LAUNDERING AND TERRORIST FINANCING RISK

Recognising that a firm does not wish to be involved with either money launderers or terrorist financiers is key to the development of an effective risk management strategy in this area. So risk management will not just be about complying with local rules and regulations but will instead also include developing risk-based assessment techniques which take account of both the risk that the relationship places on the firm and also the risk it places on the market. These two risks are of course closely aligned, with issues that are of market importance also impacting the reputation of the firm involved.

Modelling the risk based on an assessment of the inherent risk and the likelihood that a relationship may represent money laundering or terrorist financing will result in a risk prioritisation that enables enhanced due diligence and monitoring to be conducted on a structured basis in accordance with such a policy. Of course no modelling system can be 100% accurate. There will be cases of money laundering and terrorist financing that will still go undetected. However a risk-based modelling approach will ensure that the firm directs its scarce management resources to the areas of the business where they are most likely to add value.

Another key issue is how to deal with matters that become public. If there is a case of money laundering identified at your firm which is of such significance that it results in adverse publicity, then the firm needs to know the responses to make. A number of issues arise. What legally is the firm allowed to say? Just because a case has become public knowledge does not enable a firm to notify the press that a Suspicious Activity Report (or SAR) has in fact been made. Instead the firm needs to be able to make statements regarding the nature of the policies and procedures that it adopts in all cases which would also have been applied to the specific case under consideration.

If there is a criminal prosecution then the position is rather different. In such cases the firm needs to be able to demonstrate that its policies and procedures were adequate, proportionate and complied with. It is important that staff that deal with the media in such cases are appropriately trained and capable of minimising the reputational impact of the event. This will not come naturally so training for such an eventuality, including role plays, should be undertaken.

Chapter 23

MONEY LAUNDERING DETERRENCE SOFTWARE

WHAT IS MONEY LAUNDERING DETERRENCE SOFTWARE?

As part of a firm's obligations to combating money laundering, firms often decide to invest in the use of money laundering software. Anti-money laundering software is essentially a computer program designed to analyse and record customer data, and detect suspicious transactions. Some of the main providers of money laundering software (highlighting their owners, where relevant) include Actimize (NICE), Ambit (Sungard), Mantas (Oracle), Fiserv (formerly NetEconomy), Fortent (formerly Searchspace, also NICE), Norkom and SAS.

There is no single approach to the way in which such software operates, although the products do fall into two broad categories. The first is the scenario modelling approach and the second the inference-based approach.

The scenario approach

In the scenario modelling approach the software house will have considered the attributes that might identify money laundering or terrorist financing. They will then have designed a series of scenarios which they consider may represent identifiers of potential cases of money laundering. The firm then uses the software to run against a file of transactions and balances, with the software then reporting all transactions that fit the set criteria. Clearly if the criteria do not seek to check a particular attribute, then no such transactions will be identified.

The inference approach

The alternative is the inference-based products which seek to identify what might be considered as potentially high risk transactions through viewing the likelihood of money laundering based on historic data sets. They seek to parameterise the customer and transaction profiles such that transactions and relationships which appear to diverge from normality are identified.

The choice is yours!

Both solutions have their place and both have advantages and disadvantages. Whilst the scenario modeller will identify specific transactions to review, it is difficult in such products to pick up unusual transactions related to the nature of the customer.

On the other hand the inference modellers will require a much higher level of data to enable the inference system to work effectively. When such products fail to deliver it is usually due to the inability of the firm to efficiently and cost-effectively access the information that they require, or due to the problem of false positives. The inference modeller effectively reports every transaction that the firm undertakes, ranking each in terms of its likelihood of being money laundering. Accordingly even if a firm has an inference-based system it may well also need a scenario modeller to deal with the level of false reporting.

Firms will need to decide for themselves which type of solution is best suited to their purpose and business practice. Generally it is the larger firms that would choose to implement such software, although we are seeing smaller institutions starting to implement increasingly sophisticated solutions.

THE EFFECTIVENESS OF MONEY LAUNDERING DETERRENCE SOFTWARE

The effectiveness of anti-money laundering software is often debated. All money laundering deterrence software is based on programs that are dependent on data input; they then classify according to the perceived level of suspicion and inspect the data for anomalies, whether based on statistical inference or scenario. The type of anomalies picked up will include any sudden and substantial increase in funds or a large withdrawal. Clearly the effectiveness of such a system is dependent on the level of knowledge with which the system is programmed and the data availability within the firm's systems. Any other variables, which the program is unaware of, will go undetected. However, the clear benefit of money laundering deterrence software is its ability to analyse large volumes of data continuously.

If you consider the position that would exist without the use of software you will see the problem. If a bank has a large number of accounts in a number of different locations, even trying to make sure that financial sanctions legislation is complied with will become time consuming. While a manual process can easily focus on the customer acquisition process, if an error is made in this work there will be little in terms of control procedures to identify that the customer is inappropriate. Further changes to the list will need a reassessment of the customer base on a regular basis. Remember that financial sanctions must be complied with, while a firm always wishes to avoid doing business with a money launderer. The use of software consequently serves two purposes:

1. It provides a back up control to ensure that cases of inappropriate activity are identified and reviewed.
2. It also provides a defence for the firm against the claim that it should have undertaken more review procedures.

In the presence of large volumes of data and multiple locations it would be difficult for the MLRO to operate effectively in the absence of such monitoring procedures and the personal risks can be significant.

TRANSACTION MONITORING

In Chapter 19 we discussed the ongoing responsibility to monitor transactions. Clearly to enable a firm to effectively monitor customer behaviour it is important for them to maintain adequate and up-to-date transactions documentation and customer information. This is the time when firms most benefit from the use of transaction monitoring systems, although we are not aware of any jurisdiction that explicitly requires such software to be acquired.

To have an effective transaction monitoring system, generally a firm should:

- analyse system performance at a sufficiently detailed level, for example on a rule-by-rule basis, to understand the real underlying drivers of the performance results;
- set systems so they do not generate fewer alerts simply to improve performance statistics. There is a risk of "artificially" increasing the proportion of alerts that are ultimately reported as suspicious activity reports without generating an improvement in the quality and quantity of the alerts being generated;
- deploy analytical tools to identify suspicious activity that is currently not being flagged by existing rules or profile-based monitoring;
- allocate adequate resources to analysing and assessing system performance, in particular how to define how success is

measured and produce robust objective data to analyse performance against these measures;
- consistently monitor from one period to another, rather than on an intermittent basis, to ensure that performance data is not distorted by, for example, ad hoc decisions to run particular rules at different times;
- measure performance as far as possible against like-for-like comparators, e.g. peers operating in similar markets and using similar profiling and rules.

WHAT TYPE OF ACTIONS WILL BE MONITORED BY THE SOFTWARE?

The software will monitor different things and in some cases the firm is able to add specific additional matters which they wish to investigate to the software. The types of things that are likely to be reviewed include the following:

- transaction monitoring by products, customer, value or whatever a firm decides to use as a factor;
- dormant accounts that become active;
- customer transaction volumes that change by more than a set percentage;
- know your customer information which is inconsistent with customer activity using some form of statistical technique;
- the accounts that need to be subject to enhanced due diligence and the nature of such work;
- customers where there is a gap in identification verification;
- country or business risk ratings based on external information;
- politically exposed persons (PEPs) based usually on some form of external database being input into the system;
- financial sanctions monitoring, again using some form of external database;
- identification of disqualified directors or individuals where the regulator has taken action using external information sources;
- customer activity that changes in nature or appears to follow the structure of known historic money laundering cases.

This is only a subset of the types of issue that will be monitored in practice, with each product including a variety of different approaches within the single modelling approach.

THE BENEFITS OF ANTI-MONEY LAUNDERING (AML) SOFTWARE

1. AML software enables firms to easily document that they meet some of the regulatory requirements which they are obliged to do under various anti-money laundering legislation. Programs can assist firms with ongoing monitoring and record keeping as well as detecting unusual transactions.
2. The use of software can provide a defence against fines and reputational damage in case a firm is identified as being involved with a money launderer.
3. An increase in the number of cases referred to the investigation authorities, as more focused investigations enable information to be analysed thoroughly, accurately and quickly. This increases the chances that suspicious activity reports will be promptly submitted.
4. Operational costs are reduced as computer software programs streamline the investigation process with less human input being required. This potentially releases resources and employees to invest in other areas of a firm's business.
5. The use of software can improve efficiency and business control as relevant employees are given a complete view of risks which affect the business.

WHAT TYPE OF SOFTWARE IS CURRENTLY ON THE MARKET?

1. Transaction monitoring Transaction monitoring software essentially concentrates on monitoring individual transactions for the prevention and detection of money laundering. It is particularly useful for handling large volumes of complex data within financial institutions, including retail and correspondent banks. Software currently on the market generally uses comprehensive analytical techniques to scrutinise all accounts and all transactions to produce alerts most likely to result in legitimate money laundering cases. The software generally does this by analysing various factors including:

- the risk ratings of customer type, product, service, geographical area;

- detecting matches against published watch lists such as PEP lists and OFAC;
- detecting hidden relationships between family members, beneficiaries and counterparties;
- matching account activity against known money laundering scenarios;
- analysing transaction data based on type, combinations with other transactions, dollar amounts, and other relevant information to identify potentially suspicious transactions.

They really fall into two main types – the scenario approach products (e.g., Mantas, Actimize) and the inference products (e.g., SAS and Fortent).

2. Electronic identification Money laundering software which verifies electronic ID is valuable as it enables firms to verify key documents, which clients may have physically presented but which may be forged. Such software will use sophisticated software to find numerous ways of electronically authenticating the identity of customers. This may also involve using independent data sources to verify sources of information. Certain software on the market, such as Experian, can provide a score or index value to indicate the degree of confidence that an individual's identity and address are correct. Other similar identification software on the market includes Complinet and Norkom.

3. Sanctions and PEP screening software As part of a firm's know your client obligations, firms must be aware whether they are dealing with known fraudsters, terrorists or money launderers. The effect of not having sufficient systems in place is not just the threat of penalties from regulatory authorities, or the threat to national security, but also reputational damage to the firm. Sanctions and PEP screening software frequently and closely screen its customer list for individuals identified on national and international sanctions lists, to ensure that they are not unknowingly assisting the financing of terrorist activities.

Most sanctions and PEP screening solution offers will minimise 'false positives' (potential matches requiring additional manual assessment) which can usually result from automated screening solutions. Most systems will also provide a full audit trail of sanctions and PEP screening activity for compliance reporting.

SELECTING YOUR SOFTWARE

In many cases failed software implementations are due to the lack of appreciation of the differences between types of software. This is not always obvious from the company web sites, so meetings with the different vendors and discussions with successful users will be required.

One of the key stages in the selection process is the construction of the long list – that is the list of firms that will be considered for selection, regardless of the method chosen for the ultimate selection. In many cases failed selection processes result from an incomplete long list of potential suppliers that omits key product vendors.

Chartis Research published a report in February 2010 entitled Financial Crime Risk Management Systems, which includes the following analysis of key vendors (see Figure 23.1):

A typical solution is Norkom which offers the full spectrum of capabilities:

Transaction monitoring:
Detects and profiles customer and transaction activity across all products and channels.

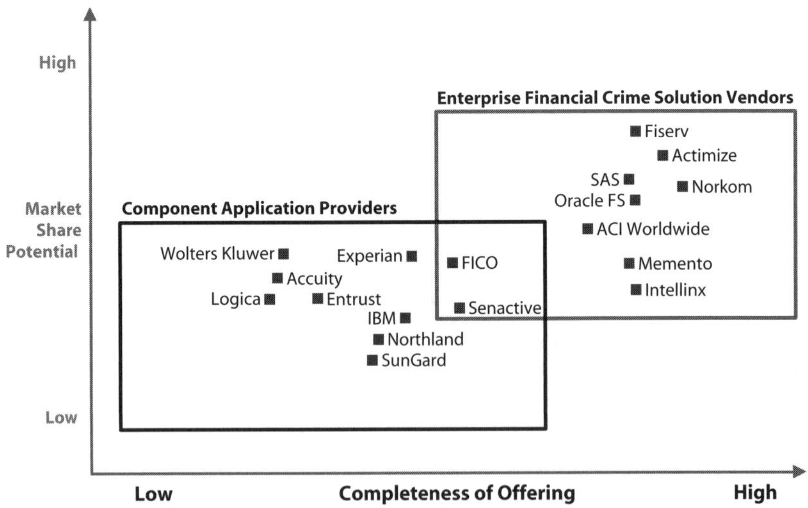

Figure 23.1 Competitive Landscape – Financial Crime Risk Management Software Vendors. *Source:* Chartis Research – Financial Crime Risk Management Systems 2010

Automated risk assessment:
Evaluates geography, product and business type, coupled with an evaluation of transactions, behaviour and static information.

Know your customer (KYC)/Customer due diligence (CDD):
Manages the customer on-boarding process through a defined sequence of steps in a due diligence workflow.

Link analysis:
Discovers hidden relationships among transactions, customers, accounts, alerts, cases, products and channels.

Integration with legacy systems and databases:
Built-in connectors accelerate integration with disparate existing systems and data sources.

AML investigative management:
Automatically triages AML alerts and provides investigative tools to manage alerts through pre-defined workflows.

Sanctions and PEP screening:
Matches names and address to a range of internal and external lists using Norkom's Watch List Management technology.

Payment and transaction filtering:
Identifies financial transactions throughout your organisation involving persons or entities contained on watch lists.

e-Filing of regulatory reports:
Automates the creation, population and filing of reports in many national and international regulatory formats.

This is only included as an example and should not be taken as any form of recommendation for the software. It does however represent the type of software that a firm would wish to consider and also includes the key elements that would be required from money laundering deterrence software.

WHAT ABOUT THE SMALLER FIRM?

For smaller firms it is unrealistic to acquire money laundering deterrence software – it is likely to be too expensive and also the firm is unlikely to maintain sufficient data to enable the software to operate effectively. Such firms will need to implement a manual form of monitoring processes and procedures to ensure that the requirements within the local jurisdiction are complied with. This would normally include a review of customer databases to ensure that sanctions and watch lists are complied with, combined with employee training to ensure that all staff are aware of their responsibilities.

By making staff aware of all of the requirements and obligations, together with the intention of such regulation, a higher level of monitoring is achievable. This however needs to be clearly documented and sufficient to enable the management of the firm to have the assurance that their firm will not be the target of money launderers and terrorist financers.

ANNEX

Transparency International's Corruption Perceptions Index measures the perceived level of public sector corruption as seen by business people and country analysts; ranging between 10 (highly clean) and 0 (highly corrupt).

Rank	*Country/Territory*	*CPI 2009 Score*	*Surveys Used*	*Confidence Range*
1	New Zealand	9.4	6	9.1–9.5
2	Denmark	9.3	6	9.1–9.5
3	Singapore	9.2	9	9.0–9.4
3	Sweden	9.2	6	9.0–9.3
5	Switzerland	9.0	6	8.9–9.1
6	Finland	8.9	6	8.4–9.4
6	Netherlands	8.9	6	8.7–9.0
8	Australia	8.7	8	8.3–9.0
8	Canada	8.7	6	8.5–9.0
8	Iceland	8.7	4	7.5–9.4
11	Norway	8.6	6	8.2–9.1
12	Hong Kong	8.2	8	7.9–8.5
12	Luxembourg	8.2	6	7.6–8.8
14	Germany	8.0	6	7.7–8.3
14	Ireland	8.0	6	7.8–8.4
16	Austria	7.9	6	7.4–8.3
17	Japan	7.7	8	7.4–8.0
17	United Kingdom	7.7	6	7.3–8.2
19	United States	7.5	8	6.9–8.0
20	Barbados	7.4	4	6.6–8.2
21	Belgium	7.1	6	6.9–7.3
22	Qatar	7.0	6	5.8–8.1
22	Saint Lucia	7.0	3	6.7–7.5
24	France	6.9	6	6.5–7.3
25	Chile	6.7	7	6.5–6.9
25	Uruguay	6.7	5	6.4–7.1
27	Cyprus	6.6	4	6.1–7.1
27	Estonia	6.6	8	6.1–6.9
27	Slovenia	6.6	8	6.3–6.9
30	United Arab Emirates	6.5	5	5.5–7.5
31	Saint Vincent and the Grenadines	6.4	3	4.9–7.5
32	Israel	6.1	6	5.4–6.7
32	Spain	6.1	6	5.5–6.6
34	Dominica	5.9	3	4.9–6.7
35	Portugal	5.8	6	5.5–6.2
35	Puerto Rico	5.8	4	5.2–6.3
37	Botswana	5.6	6	5.1–6.3
37	Taiwan	5.6	9	5.4–5.9

Rank	Country/Territory	CPI 2009 Score	Surveys Used	Confidence Range
39	Brunei Darussalam	5.5	4	4.7–6.4
39	Oman	5.5	5	4.4–6.5
39	Korea (South)	5.5	9	5.3–5.7
42	Mauritius	5.4	6	5.0–5.9
43	Costa Rica	5.3	5	4.7–5.9
43	Macau	5.3	3	3.3–6.9
45	Malta	5.2	4	4.0–6.2
46	Bahrain	5.1	5	4.2–5.8
46	Cape Verde	5.1	3	3.3–7.0
46	Hungary	5.1	8	4.6–5.7
49	Bhutan	5.0	4	4.3–5.6
49	Jordan	5.0	7	3.9–6.1
49	Poland	5.0	8	4.5–5.5
52	Czech Republic	4.9	8	4.3–5.6
52	Lithuania	4.9	8	4.4–5.4
54	Seychelles	4.8	3	3.0–6.7
55	South Africa	4.7	8	4.3–4.9
56	Latvia	4.5	6	4.1–4.9
56	Malaysia	4.5	9	4.0–5.1
56	Namibia	4.5	6	3.9–5.1
56	Samoa	4.5	3	3.3–5.3
56	Slovakia	4.5	8	4.1–4.9
61	Cuba	4.4	3	3.5–5.1
61	Turkey	4.4	7	3.9–4.9
63	Italy	4.3	6	3.8–4.9
63	Saudi Arabia	4.3	5	3.1–5.3
65	Tunisia	4.2	6	3.0–5.5
66	Croatia	4.1	8	3.7–4.5
66	Georgia	4.1	7	3.4–4.7
66	Kuwait	4.1	5	3.2–5.1
69	Ghana	3.9	7	3.2–4.6
69	Montenegro	3.9	5	3.5–4.4
71	Bulgaria	3.8	8	3.2–4.5
71	FYR Macedonia	3.8	6	3.4–4.2
71	Greece	3.8	6	3.2–4.3
71	Romania	3.8	8	3.2–4.3
75	Brazil	3.7	7	3.3–4.3
75	Colombia	3.7	7	3.1–4.3
75	Peru	3.7	7	3.4–4.1
75	Suriname	3.7	3	3.0–4.7
79	Burkina Faso	3.6	7	2.8–4.4
79	China	3.6	9	3.0–4.2
79	Swaziland	3.6	3	3.0–4.7
79	Trinidad and Tobago	3.6	4	3.0–4.3

Rank	Country/Territory	CPI 2009 Score	Surveys Used	Confidence Range
83	Serbia	3.5	6	3.3–3.9
84	El Salvador	3.4	5	3.0–3.8
84	Guatemala	3.4	5	3.0–3.9
84	India	3.4	10	3.2–3.6
84	Panama	3.4	5	3.1–3.7
84	Thailand	3.4	9	3.0–3.8
89	Lesotho	3.3	6	2.8–3.8
89	Malawi	3.3	7	2.7–3.9
89	Mexico	3.3	7	3.2–3.5
89	Moldova	3.3	6	2.7–4.0
89	Morocco	3.3	6	2.8–3.9
89	Rwanda	3.3	4	2.9–3.7
95	Albania	3.2	6	3.0–3.3
95	Vanuatu	3.2	3	2.3–4.7
97	Liberia	3.1	3	1.9–3.8
97	Sri Lanka	3.1	7	2.8–3.4
99	Bosnia and Herzegovina	3.0	7	2.6–3.4
99	Dominican Republic	3.0	5	2.9–3.2
99	Jamaica	3.0	5	2.8–3.3
99	Madagascar	3.0	7	2.8–3.2
99	Senegal	3.0	7	2.5–3.6
99	Tonga	3.0	3	2.6–3.3
99	Zambia	3.0	7	2.8–3.2
106	Argentina	2.9	7	2.6–3.1
106	Benin	2.9	6	2.3–3.4
106	Gabon	2.9	3	2.6–3.1
106	Gambia	2.9	5	1.6–4.0
106	Niger	2.9	5	2.7–3.0
111	Algeria	2.8	6	2.5–3.1
111	Djibouti	2.8	4	2.3–3.2
111	Egypt	2.8	6	2.6–3.1
111	Indonesia	2.8	9	2.4–3.2
111	Kiribati	2.8	3	2.3–3.3
111	Mali	2.8	6	2.4–3.2
111	Sao Tome and Principe	2.8	3	2.4–3.3
111	Solomon Islands	2.8	3	2.3–3.3
111	Togo	2.8	5	1.9–3.9
120	Armenia	2.7	7	2.6–2.8
120	Bolivia	2.7	6	2.4–3.1
120	Ethiopia	2.7	7	2.4–2.9
120	Kazakhstan	2.7	7	2.1–3.3
120	Mongolia	2.7	7	2.4–3.0
120	Vietnam	2.7	9	2.4–3.1
126	Eritrea	2.6	4	1.6–3.8

Rank	*Country/Territory*	*CPI 2009 Score*	*Surveys Used*	*Confidence Range*
126	Guyana	2.6	4	2.5–2.7
126	Syria	2.6	5	2.2–2.9
126	Tanzania	2.6	7	2.4–2.9
130	Honduras	2.5	6	2.2–2.8
130	Lebanon	2.5	3	1.9–3.1
130	Libya	2.5	6	2.2–2.8
130	Maldives	2.5	4	1.8–3.2
130	Mauritania	2.5	7	2.0–3.3
130	Mozambique	2.5	7	2.3–2.8
130	Nicaragua	2.5	6	2.3–2.7
130	Nigeria	2.5	7	2.2–2.7
130	Uganda	2.5	7	2.1–2.8
139	Bangladesh	2.4	7	2.0–2.8
139	Belarus	2.4	4	2.0–2.8
139	Pakistan	2.4	7	2.1–2.7
139	Philippines	2.4	9	2.1–2.7
143	Azerbaijan	2.3	7	2.0–2.6
143	Comoros	2.3	3	1.6–3.3
143	Nepal	2.3	6	2.0–2.6
146	Cameroon	2.2	7	1.9–2.6
146	Ecuador	2.2	5	2.0–2.5
146	Kenya	2.2	7	1.9–2.5
146	Russia	2.2	8	1.9–2.4
146	Sierra Leone	2.2	5	1.9–2.4
146	Timor-Leste	2.2	5	1.8–2.6
146	Ukraine	2.2	8	2.0–2.6
146	Zimbabwe	2.2	7	1.7–2.8
154	Côte d'Ivoire	2.1	7	1.8–2.4
154	Papua New Guinea	2.1	5	1.7–2.5
154	Paraguay	2.1	5	1.7–2.5
154	Yemen	2.1	4	1.6–2.5
158	Cambodia	2.0	8	1.8–2.2
158	Central African Republic	2.0	4	1.9–2.2
158	Laos	2.0	4	1.6–2.6
158	Tajikistan	2.0	8	1.6–2.5
162	Angola	1.9	5	1.8–1.9
162	Congo Brazzaville	1.9	5	1.6–2.1
162	Democratic Republic of Congo	1.9	5	1.7–2.1
162	Guinea-Bissau	1.9	3	1.8–2.0
162	Kyrgyzstan	1.9	7	1.8–2.1
162	Venezuela	1.9	7	1.8–2.0
168	Burundi	1.8	6	1.6–2.0

Rank	*Country/Territory*	*CPI 2009 Score*	*Surveys Used*	*Confidence Range*
168	Equatorial Guinea	1.8	3	1.6–1.9
168	Guinea	1.8	5	1.7–1.8
168	Haiti	1.8	3	1.4–2.3
168	Iran	1.8	3	1.7–1.9
168	Turkmenistan	1.8	4	1.7–1.9
174	Uzbekistan	1.7	6	1.5–1.8
175	Chad	1.6	6	1.5–1.7
176	Iraq	1.5	3	1.2–1.8
176	Sudan	1.5	5	1.4–1.7
178	Myanmar	1.4	3	0.9–1.8
179	Afghanistan	1.3	4	1.0–1.5
180	Somalia	1.1	3	0.9–1.4

Source: Transparency International (2009). Reproduced with permission.

INDEX